Hal Leonard Guitar
RECORDED VERSIONS™
With Notes & Tab

ERIC CLA CROSSROADS VOL. 2

MW00595517

Transcriptions by Larry Giannecchini

Cover and text illustrations by Ron Wood
Essay by Anthony DeCurtis

HAL•LEONARD CORPORATION
7777 W. BLUEMOUND RD. P.O. BOX 13819 MILWAUKEE, WI 53213

ERIC CLAPTON

A LIFE AT THE CROSSROADS

by Anthony DeCurtis

Over the past twenty-five years Eric Clapton's extraordinary career has traced a dramatic progression marked by musical pioneering, restless shifts of direction, spiritual awakenings, backsliding and, at one point, a total retreat into isolation. Clapton's mysterious, internally determined moves from budding pop star to purist blues man to rock guitar hero to laid-back troubadour have challenged the faithful and won new converts at every turn.

Through all the personal and artistic upheavals, part of Eric Clapton has consistently remained detached and calm, as if he accepted in his heart that he was destined for such shocks — and that acceptance brought a certain peace. At the same time he has maintained a fierce, private idealism about his playing. "My driving philosophy about making music," he told *Rolling Stone* in 1974, "is that you can reduce it all down to one note if that note is played with the right kind of feeling and with the right kind of sincerity."

It makes sense, then, that Robert Johnson's tough, transcendent masterpiece, "Crossroads," has become Clapton's signature song. On the path of life, crossroads are where the breakdowns and breakthroughs come, where danger and adventure lie. As he has forged and disbanded musical alliances, altered his sound and his look, pursued and dodged fame, Eric Clapton has brought himself to the crossroads and proven himself time and time again.

Clapton's bold search for his own identity is the source both of his enormous artistic achievement and his inner strife. That search acquired its momentum in the earliest years of his life. Clapton was born on March 30th, 1945 in Ripley, a small village about thirty miles outside — and a universe away from — London. His mother raised him until he was two years old, at which point she moved abroad, leaving him in the loving hands of her mother and stepfather.

The elderly couple was indulgent of Eric — they bought him his first guitar on an installment plan when he was in his teens — but the stigma of being born out of wedlock in a small town made a forceful impression on him. The "secret" of Clapton's illegitimacy was a secret only from him. "I was raised by my grandparents, thinking that they were my parents, up until I was nine years old," Clapton explained to J. D. Considine in *Musician* in 1986. "That's when the shock came up, when I found out — from outside sources — that they weren't my parents, they were my grandparents. I went into a kind of . . . shock, which lasted through my teens, really, and started to turn me into the kind of person I am now."

Clapton was more pointed in Ray Coleman's authorized biography, *Clapton!*, published in 1985, about how hard it was to learn the truth about his background. "My feeling of a lack of identity started to rear its head then," he told Coleman. "And it explains a lot of my behavior throughout my life; it changed my outlook and my physical appearance so much. Because I still don't know who I am."

Like so many rockers, Clapton did a brief stint in art school — the Kingston College of Art, in his case. His formal education got derailed, however, when he was

about sixteen and began to make the bohemian scene in London, where he discovered folk-blues. Eventually he would go on to play acoustic gigs in coffee-houses and pubs, accompanied by a vocalist and doing tunes by Big Bill Broonzy, Ramblin' Jack Elliott and Blind Boy Fuller.

Another revelation struck around that time, as well. "Every Friday night, there would be a meeting at someone's house, and people would turn up with the latest imported records from the States," Clapton recalled in a 1985 *Rolling Stone* interview with Robert Palmer. "And shortly, someone showed up with that Chess album, *The Best of Muddy Waters*, and something by Howlin' Wolf. And that was it for me. Then I sort of took a step back, discovered Robert Johnson and made the connection to Muddy." In later days, Clapton would come to refer to Muddy Waters as his "father." And Johnson's haunted country blues affected Clapton so deeply that he would tell Dan Forte in *Guitar Player* more than two decades later, "Both of the Robert Johnson albums (*King of the Delta Blues Singers*, Volumes 1 and 2) actually cover all of my desires musically. Every angle of expression and every emotion is expressed on both of those albums."

The first band Clapton joined was the fledgling R&B outfit, the Roosters. The Roosters would last only a few months, from March to October of 1963, according to rock historian Pete Frame. But during that period the band's bassist, Tom McGuinness, who later played with Manfred Mann and McGuinness Flint, turned Clapton on to blues guitarist Freddie King's instrumental "Hideaway," and another influential figure entered Clapton's pantheon. Playing John Lee Hooker and Muddy Waters' tunes with the Roosters sharpened Clapton's playing, according to the band's pianist Ben Palmer, one of the guitarist's oldest friends. "It was immediately obvious that he was something that none of the rest of us were," Palmer says in *Clapton!* "And he had a fluency and command that seemed endless. The telling point was that he didn't mind taking solos, which people of our standard often did because we weren't up to it."

Following an extremely short stay with the pop band Casey Jones and the Engineers — headed by Liverpool singer Brian Cassar, who was trying to cash in on the record-company signing spree in the wake of the Beatles' success — Clapton joined the seminal Sixties band, the Yardbirds, in October of 1963. In their early days the Yardbirds — who, in addition to Clapton, consisted of vocalist Keith Relf, guitarist Chris Dreja, bassist Paul Samwell-Smith and drummer Jim McCarty — were an exuberant London R&B band that covered tunes like John Lee Hooker's "Boom Boom" and Billy Boy Arnold's "I Wish You Would."

On "I Ain't Got You" — and in his brief solo on the catchy New Orleans novelty, "A Certain Girl" — Clapton flashes the biting, fiercely articulate phrasing characteristic of his best playing. But in general Clapton was inhibited by the Yardbirds' harmonica-driven rave-up style. Despite his youth, Clapton was sufficiently confident of his musical tastes to become disgruntled when the Yardbirds, at the urging of manager Giorgio Gomelsky, edged away from the blues in order to pursue pop success. Clapton left the group by mutual agreement shortly after they recorded Graham Gouldman's "For Your Love" in quest of a hit.

Splitting from the Yardbirds on the brink of their commercial breakthrough was the first time Clapton displayed his willingness to pursue his own musical vision at whatever the cost — and it was far from the last. However high-minded and necessary such decisions were, Clapton is not beyond questioning them to a degree, in retrospect. "I took it all far too seriously," he states in *Clapton!* "Perhaps if I'd been able to temper it, I might not have been so frustrated . . . I still take it too seriously, in terms of relationships and being able to get on with other musicians. I'm far too judgemental, and in those days I was a complete purist. If it wasn't black music, it was rubbish."

Of course, seriousness about black music was hardly a problem during Clapton's tenure with John Mayall's Bluesbreakers in 1965 and 1966. A keyboardist with a vocal style derived from Mose Allison and Freddie King, Mayall was twelve years Clapton's senior and the father of the British blues scene. Mayall's Bluesbreakers were the proving ground for a host of ambitious young musicians in the mid to late Sixties, including Jack Bruce, Mick Taylor, Peter Green, Aynsley Dunbar, John McVie and Mick Fleetwood.

Clapton raided Mayall's vast collection of singles, and the two men thrived on each other's enthusiasm, as is evidenced by the raw Chicago blues power of their duet on "Lonely Years" and the spry assurance of their instrumental jam, "Bernard Jenkins." Though barely into his twenties, Clapton shaped an aggressive, tonally rich playing style with the Bluesbreakers. Drawing on Freddie King, Otis Rush and Buddy Guy in a way that blended respect with his own precocious mastery, Clapton unleashed some of the finest blues guitar playing of his generation on the 1966 *Bluesbreakers — John Mayall with Eric Clapton* LP. In addition, Clapton sang his first lead vocal on that record, a spare, eloquent reading of Robert Johnson's "Ramblin' On My Mind" that captures all that song's edgy amalgam of anguish and submerged threat.

Clapton's scorching club performances in London during his time with Mayall — represented in this collection by his ignition of Billy Myles' "Have You Ever Loved a Woman," with Jack Bruce on bass — quickly established a cult following for the young guitarist. "Clapton Is God" graffiti began appearing around the city, defining a central tenet of the Clapton mythology to this day. And though the comparisons with God would prove to be a hellhound on Clapton's trail, he understandably received the adulation more positively at first.

"My vanity was incredibly boosted by that 'God' thing," Clapton says in Coleman's biography. "I didn't think there was anyone around at that time doing what I was doing, playing the blues as straight as me. I was trying to do it absolutely according to its rules. Oh yeah, I was very confident. I didn't think there was anybody as good."

However appealing, the adulation did not prevent Clapton from taking a three-month break from the Bluesbreakers in 1965, and it was during that period that Jack Bruce joined the band. Playing with Bruce upon his return spun Clapton's head around. Bruce's jazz background gave his playing an improvisational flair, and Clapton, who, despite his own purist impulses, had been feeling somewhat constrained in Mayall's strict blues format, felt a new sense of freedom. "Most of what we were doing with Mayall was imitating the records we got, but Jack had something else," Clapton told *Rolling Stone*, "he had no reverence for what we were doing, and so he was composing new parts as he went along playing. I literally had never heard that before, and it took me someplace else. I thought, well, if he could do that, and I could, and we could get a drummer . . . I could be Buddy Guy with a composing bass player. And that's how Cream came about."

Formed in 1966, Cream's impact on the world of pop music was immense. Rock bands to that point had played almost exclusively before crowds of screaming teeny-boppers — a major reason why live performance was beginning to seem pointless to bands whose music and ideas were becoming more sophisticated. Discussing rock and roll in musical terms was a joke to the mainstream media, and alternative media had not yet sprung up. Cream was a primary catalyst in transforming rock and roll into music that could be performed in concert before adults and analyzed with the same rigor that blues or jazz could be. The declaration implicit in the band's name was itself a demand to be taken seriously. In Coleman's terse summary, "They made musicianship hip." Clapton forever defined the role of guitar hero at this point, and with Bruce on bass and the redoubtable Ginger Baker on drums, Cream defined the power trio.

In their range and power, Cream forced a dichotomy between the studio and the stage. In the studio, the band was something like a later evolution of the Yardbirds. They could contain hip innovations within pop-song structures, as on "I Feel Free"; rework the blues, as on Willie Dixon's "Spoonful" and the Albert King-derived "Strange Brew"; journey into psychedelic wonderland, as on "Tales of Brave Ulysses" and "White Room"; or simply cut a radio-perfect, guitar-charged hit like "Sunshine of Your Love."

Live, however, Cream was essentially a rock-and-roll jazz band. Songs became thematic statements that provided the occasion for lengthy improvisational jams, with Baker and Bruce muscling each other into unexplored territory as Clapton wailed and roared above them. The propulsive live version of "Crossroads" included here is a Cream classic, and a masterpiece of concision — edited, as it was, by engineer Tom Dowd for the *Wheels of Fire* album — compared to the much longer renditions the band typically fired up.

The hero-worship Clapton had inspired when he was with the Bluesbreakers reached a fever pitch with Cream. The pressures of the inordinate praise heaped upon him, the wild improvisational competitiveness of Cream's gigs, and the fighting that resulted from Bruce and Baker's inability to get along gradually took their toll on Clapton.

"All during Cream I was riding high on the 'Clapton is God' myth that had been started up,"

Clapton told Robert Palmer. "Then we got our first kind of bad review, which, funnily enough, was in *Rolling Stone*. The magazine ran an interview with us in which we were really praising ourselves, and it was followed by a review that said how boring and repetitious our performance had been. And it was true! . . . I immediately decided that that was the end of the band."

Cream split up in November of 1968, about six months after that review appeared, and Clapton began jamming with Steve Winwood, the keyboardist and sterling R&B vocalist who had made his own youthful mark with the Spencer Davis Group and Traffic. The two men had played and recorded together two years earlier, and Clapton admired Winwood's tunefulness as a singer and songwriter — qualities that stood in sharp relief after the jazz-rock experimentalism of Cream.

But, given their musical pedigrees, Clapton and Winwood were hot commercial commodities. Because all three of its members had been eminent figures on the British scene, Cream had begun a trend toward supergroups, and the prospect of Winwood and Clapton teaming up was too hot a proposition for the business people to resist. What began idyllically with Clapton and Winwood jamming together at their homes in the country and searching for new musical directions quickly became a cash cow. Ginger Baker and Rick Grech, bassist of the English folk-rock band Family, were recruited as the rhythm section, and Blind Faith was born.

Formed in early 1969, Blind Faith debuted at a huge outdoor concert in London's Hyde Park in June of that year, recorded one album and then launched an arena tour in America. The band broke up in late 1969, and Clapton offered this bluntly honest obituary in *Rolling Stone* shortly afterwards: "We didn't rehearse enough, we didn't get to know each other enough, we didn't go through enough trials and tribulations before the big time came."

Still, the *Blind Faith* album, recorded in February, May and June of 1969 had a number of splendid moments. Steve Winwood's searching "Can't Find My Way Home," with Clapton on acoustic guitar, is a fine example of the kind of melodic, song-centered work Clapton was becoming more interested in after Cream. Among the earliest tunes Blind Faith laid down in the studio, Clapton's "Presence of the Lord" was the first non-instrumental song he ever recorded that he wrote fully on his own. It was also the first of the hymn-like spiritual songs of faith that would become a staple of his work in years to come.

The opening act on the Blind Faith tour of America in 1969 was a rocking R&B band led by Delaney and Bonnie Bramlett. Delaney and Bonnie played a loose, engaging blend of the full range of American soul music, and their unassuming, good-hearted shows seemed to Clapton a sharp contrast to Blind Faith's headline gigs. Clapton began spending more and more time with Delaney and his band, traveling from gig to gig on their tour bus and popping up on stage during their sets. In a 1970 interview in *Rolling Stone*, Clapton recalled that "on certain nights I'd get up there and play tambourine with Delaney's group and enjoy it more

than playing with Blind Faith . . . And by then I kind of got this crusade going for Delaney's group. I wanted to bring them over to England."

Blind Faith splintered once their blitz of America ended. At that point, Clapton not only sponsored a tour of England for Delaney and Bonnie, he played guitar with the band and recorded the infectiously upbeat single, "Comin' Home," with them. A live album from the tour was released later. More important, however, Delaney was the agent of a significant emotional breakthrough for Clapton.

Since about 1968, Clapton had been growing bored with virtuoso musicianship and more interested in songs that had clearly delineated structures and put across a pleasing groove. The Band's *Music from Big Pink*, which came out that year, made a striking impression on him and fueled his dissatisfaction with Cream. Discussing Cream's break-up in *Rolling Stone* in 1974, Clapton said "another interesting factor was that I got the tapes of *Music from Big Pink* and I thought, well, this is what I want to play — not extended solos and maestro bullshit but just good funky songs." The concise, melodic "Badge," which Clapton co-wrote for Cream's *Goodbye* album with George Harrison, who also plays guitar on the song, was one product of this interest. Forming a band with Steve Winwood and serving as a guitar-slinger side-man to Delaney and Bonnie were other manifestations of it.

Yet despite his strong performances on "Ramblin' on My Mind," "Crossroads" and other tracks, Clapton was still extremely shy about his singing. Clapton told Robert Palmer that on the night he and Delaney met, "Delaney looked straight into my eyes and told me I had a gift to sing and that if I didn't sing, God would take it away. I said, 'No, man, I can't sing.' But he said, 'Yes, you can.' . . . That night we started talking about me making a solo album, with his band."

When Delaney and Bonnie's tour of England ended, the two men went into the studio in Los Angeles and began work on Clapton's first solo album, *Eric Clapton*. Delaney's influence on the record was considerable. He produced the album — which includes the joyful "Blues Power" and the fiery "Let It Rain" — and supplied most of the players from his own band. His hand is especially evident on the alternative version of J. J. Cale's "After Midnight" — which Delaney mixed and which features a horn section that does not appear on the LP track. With Delaney's encouragement, Clapton emerged as a front man for the first time since he had been propelled into superstardom with Cream. Clapton wrote or co-wrote eight of the eleven tunes on the record, sang all the lead vocals and played crisply and spiritedly. He was now ready to put together a band of his own.

When Clapton learned that three members of Delaney's band — keyboardist Bobby Whitlock, bassist Carl Radle and drummer Jim Gordon — had had a falling out with their boss and were available, he scooped them up. The band came together and did their first recording while they were all working on the sessions for George Harrison's *All Things Must Pass* album, which Phil Spector was producing. They recorded a blistering version of "Tell the Truth" —

backed with the salacious "Roll It Over," featuring Harrison and Dave Mason on guitars — as a single, with Spector at the board. But, at the band's insistence, the track was recalled within days of its released.

Still ambivalent about his rock-star status, Clapton avoided using his own name and debuted his new band at a benefit concert in London as Derek and the Dominos. And rather than play large halls, he booked a club tour of England for their first trip out. As undisputed leader of the Dominos, Clapton was able both to play songs he felt comfortable with and to stretch out in solos when he desired. "It wasn't until I formed Derek and the Dominos and we played live that I was aware of being able to do exactly what I wanted and was happy with it," Clapton told Dan Forte in 1985. But Clapton's musical satisfaction contrasted with the emotional pain he was experiencing. He had fallen in love with Pattie Boyd Harrison, who at the time was married to his best friend, George Harrison. With the turmoil of a classic blues triangle worthy of Robert Johnson exploding inside him, Clapton left for Miami with the Dominos to make *Layla*.

Layla was recorded with legendary producer Tom Dowd under the most extreme conditions. Critic Robert Palmer visited the sessions and later recalled, "There was a lot of dope around, especially heroin, and when I showed up, everyone was just spread out on the carpet, nodded out." Shortly after the band arrived in Miami, Dowd took them to see the Allman Brothers, and Duane Allman was invited to play slide guitar on the album. Allman also teamed up with Clapton for a duet on Little Walter's "Mean Old World," which was not included on the LP.

Driven creatively by his new band, the formidable playing of Allman and his own romantic agony, Clapton poured all he had into *Layla*'s title track, which was inspired by a Persian love story he had read, *The Story of Layla and Majnun* by Nizami. The song's extended lyrical coda was composed independently by drummer Jim Gordon on piano, and Gordon had to be convinced to allow the piece to be tacked onto "Layla."

After completing *Layla*, Derek and the Dominos launched a tour of America, from which the previously unreleased live versions of "Key to the Highway" and "Crossroads" — in a more churning, exploratory rendition than the one recorded with Cream — included in this collection are taken. The band then returned to England, and in April and May of 1971 attempted to record a second studio album — five tracks of which are presented in this collection for the first time: "One More Chance," Arthur Crudup's "Mean Old Frisco," the instrumental "Snake Lake Blues," a cover of Willie Dixon's "Evil," and an uncompleted studio version of "Got to Get Better in a Little While," which the band performed live on the album, *Derek and the Dominos in Concert*. In his 1985 interview in *Rolling Stone* Clapton told Robert Palmer that the sessions for a follow-up LP to Layla "broke down halfway through because of the paranoia and the tension. And the band just . . . dissolved."

Once the Dominos broke up, Clapton's drug dependence worsened and kept him virtually a prisoner in his home for the rest of 1971 — though he did emerge to play at George Harrison's Concert for Bangladesh that summer — and much of the following year. During this period he felt both personally and emotionally adrift, and the long-standing identity issues arose once again. "The end of the Dominos came too soon, and that left me very high and dry as to what I was supposed to be," he told *Guitar Player* in 1985. "I'd been this anonymous person up until that time. It was difficult for me to come to terms with the fact that it was *me*, that I was on my own again."

Part of that difficulty may have resulted from the origins of Derek and the Dominos in Clapton's own psychic need. Despite the enormous satisfactions the band brought him, Clapton told *Musician* that Derek and the Dominos were "a make-believe band. We were all hiding inside it. Derek & the Dominos — the whole thing was . . . assumed. So it couldn't last. I had to come out and admit that I was being me. I mean, being Derek was a cover for the fact that I was trying to steal someone else's wife. That was one of the reasons for doing it, so that I could write the song, and even use another name for Pattie. So Derek and Layla — it wasn't real at all."

Clapton's good friend Pete Townshend of the Who organized a concert at London's Rainbow Theatre in January of 1973 to create some momentum for the guitarist's return to action. Clapton played at the highly emotional show with Townshend, Ron Wood and Steve Winwood, and later that year took an acupuncture cure

to end his drug addiction. Once that problem was behind him, Clapton contacted Tom Dowd and returned to Miami to record *461 Ocean Boulevard*.

Featuring a band of American musicians, including Carl Radle, brought together by Dowd, *461 Ocean Boulevard* is Clapton's great comeback LP. Appropriately, it opens with "Motherless Children," a traditional tune whose rollicking energy in Clapton's slide-guitar version counterpoints its relevance to the circumstances of his early life. The deeply felt "Let It Grow" finds Clapton once again "standing at the crossroads," and this time making a choice to affirm life, love and, by extension, his ability to reach within himself and create art. And *461 Ocean Boulevard* contained Clapton's cover of Bob Marley's "I Shot the Sheriff" — represented here in a tougher, more expansive live rendition from the band's December 5th, 1974 concert at the Hammersmith Odeon in London — which exposed millions of Americans to reggae music for the first time when it became a Number One hit. During the *461 Ocean Boulevard* sessions at Criteria Studios in Miami, Clapton also recorded Jimmy Reed's insinuatingly seductive "Ain't That Lovin' You" with Dave Mason on guitar — a previously unreleased track included in this collection.

461 Ocean Boulevard re-established Clapton in both critical and commercial terms, but it also ushered in the phase of his career that engendered concern in many of his longest-standing followers. In their concentration on songwriting, vocals and melody, *461 Ocean Boulevard* and the nine studio LPs that have followed it de-emphasize the pyrotechnic guitar work that characterized Clapton's tracks with the Bluesbreakers, Cream and Derek and the Dominos — though there's certainly no shortage of excellent playing. Working with a variety of producers — including Dowd, Glyn Johns and Phil Collins — Clapton alternated between American and British bands, experimenting with a wide variety of sounds and styles. Conventional pop songs and laid-back ballads of broad appeal appeared on those records and jarred the sensibilities of some fans.

A number of issues are important for understanding Clapton's music since 1974. One is that, while Clapton is still gripped by the blues and inclined to explore his favorite standards at length in live performance (note his probing reading of Otis Rush's "Double Trouble" in this collection), that impulse is no longer single and all-consuming. Since the latter days of Cream, the thrust of Clapton's music has been towards melody, and the artists that have interested him — the Band, Bob Dylan, Bob Marley, J. J. Cale, country singer Don Williams — are often more subtle than they are explosive. Taken together those artists and Clapton's blues idols are the influences behind his most notable work of the late Seventies and Eighties.

In 1985 Clapton spoke of a desire he felt during the Seventies "to be more of a composer of melodic tunes rather than just a player, which was very unpopular with a lot of people." The remark echoes something he said eleven years earlier, in expressing admiration for Stevie Wonder: "I think when it comes down to it, I always go for singers. I don't buy an album because I

like the lead guitar. I always like the human voice most of all." The greatest blues guitar playing, after all, is modeled on the sound of the human voice.

Blues, country, folk, rock and pop have come to share a place in Clapton's music. He offered a sensitive reading of Elmore James' "The Sky Is Crying" on *There's One in Every Crowd* (in addition to recording James' "(When Things Go Wrong) It Hurts Me Too" during the sessions for that album), and, in a live cut from 1977 included here, did an upbeat take on "Further On Up the Road," which over the years has become one of his signature tunes. Members of the Band were a prominent presence on the gently rolling *No Reason to Cry* album, which featured Clapton's optimistic "Hello Old Friend." Bob Dylan appeared on that record as well, sharing the vocal on his enigmatic song, "Sign Language."

Clapton also turned in fine versions of Dylan's "Knockin' on Heaven's Door" — another expression of the guitarist's spiritual side — and his swinging "If I Don't Be There By Morning." J. J. Cale's ominously enticing "Cocaine," included on Clapton's 1978 multi-platinum LP, *Slowhand*, has proven to be one of Clapton's most popular tunes, and Clapton's own catchy hit, "Lay Down Sally," from that same album, owes a clear debt to Cale. The affectionate "Wonderful Tonight," also from *Slowhand*, was simply born of Clapton's wish to write a love song.

Clapton's popularity as a live performer has consistently grown over the past ten years, and the videos and the pop-oriented LPs he has made with producer Phil Collins — *Behind the Sun* and *August* (which was co-produced by Tom Dowd) — have brought his music to a younger audience eager to learn about his past. He composed a soundtrack for the BBC television series *Edge of Darkness*, which won prestigious BAFTA and Ivor Novello awards in Great Britain, and for the film *Lethal Weapon*. He contributed songs to films, including "Heaven Is One Step Away" for *Back to the Future* and two tracks for *The Color of Money*, directed by Martin Scorsese.

As a blues prodigy, Clapton built a commanding reputation very early in his twenties. By the time he was thirty he had, like many masters, become intrigued by simplicity — the one-note philosophy. The calm that he felt at his core — through the times of revolutionary innovation, through the drugs and the cure, through heartbreak and happiness, at the crossroads and further on up the road — finally entered his music.

In *Musician* in 1986 Clapton said, "I think that the ultimate guitar hero should be a dispenser of wisdom, as well as anything else.... that's the one thing I will say that I'm still striving after, outside of perfection as a musician: the attainment of wisdom, in any amount."

If wisdom can be reflected in the creation of a superbly accomplished body of work and in the defeat of personal adversity, Eric Clapton has already achieved the major portion of his goal. And the remainder has not escaped him. It awaits him — and us, his audience — at the spectacular series of crossroads to come.

— Anthony DeCurtis
Senior Writer
Rolling Stone

ERIC CLAPTON'S GUITAR STYLE

By Larry Giannecchini (Transcriber)

Clearly, the key description of the CROSSROADS Recordings 3 and 4 that comprise this volume is "maturity." Here, Clapton finds fertile ground from seeds planted in his earlier period (see CROSSROADS Volume I, featuring Recordings 1 and 2). There's a departure from the lengthily improvised solos and his arrival at song-oriented composition. Nevertheless, the urgent and aggressive Clapton trademark is stamped on every cut.

Homage must also be paid to the recording industry that matured concurrently with Clapton's growth. The fidelity on Recordings 3 and 4 is greatly improved. The multitracking

process, enabling the layering and overdubbing of parts, allowed for a technically more advanced realization of the compositions.

Volume II opens with the Delaney and Bonnie tune, COMIN' HOME. Clapton chose the stringy, dewy, Telecaster sound associated with country pickers. Note the double-stop bends that begin and end well over a full step. The next three cuts are from the ERIC CLAPTON album. Check out the slapback echo effect on the guitar lines in AFTER MIDNIGHT. With the enlistment of Stephen Stills on guitar, LET IT RAIN captures the Buffalo Springfield sound. Listen for the blistering repetition of pentatonic triplet slurs in Clapton's solo. The collaboration on ROLL IT OVER with George Harrison is down and dirty and features Clapton's x-rated slide/wah artistry. There is a definite Beatle sound in the bridge (incidently, the album from which this song is taken was produced by Phil Spector). More Beatles' influence surfaces on LET IT GROW. Twangy single-note *arpeggiation* of the chord progression, an electric slide duet into the solo section, an acoustic slide guitar solo and repetition of the chord progression with building textures are typical "Beatlsms" of the time.

LAYLA from the Derek and the Dominos period is a masterpiece of texture. The guitar tracks are layered in octaves, parallel sixths and slide melodies. The result is delicately transparent, yet powerful. What can be said of the Clapton-Allman slide guitar duet? *Simply stunning!* The middle solo interlude is played over the highest frets and pickups on the guitar.

On MEAN OLD WORLD, Clapton and Duane Allman are slapping and sliding in authentic Mississippi blues style on acoustic guitars. A similar feel plus rhythm section is heard on MEAN OLD FRISCO. ONE MORE CHANCE echoes with the feel of Appalachian folk music via the dobro and banjo trio interlude.

In the *guitar-and-amp-set-to-growl* category are CROSSROADS, AIN'T THAT LOVIN' YOU and GOT TO GET BETTER IN A LITTLE WHILE. The latter features an extended snarling solo that incorporates string bends and wah techniques that produce a talking guitar vocabulary. Blazing sixteenth note pentatonic flurries fly through the solo.

EVIL has more slide-wah mastery over rockabilly underpinnings. KEY TO THE HIGHWAY and SNAKE LAKE BLUES from Derek and the Dominos showcase Clapton's expertise in playing the blues. Like his mentors, B.B. King and Freddie King, Clapton utilizes pre-bends, bends, bend releases and bluesy vibrato. His eloquent dynamics communicate soulful depth as phrases disappear into thin air.

I SHOT THE SHERIFF reveals Clapton's appreciation for reggae. Listen for his muted "steel drum" guitar fills. His hard pick attacks while palm muting, and his electronic slap echo produce this timbre. Record 4 closes with BETTER MAKE IT THROUGH TODAY, an understated blues in alternating B major and B minor.

CONCERNING NOTATION

In an effort to present a more accessible and comprehensible format in these transcriptions, certain aspects of phrasing have been simplified. You will notice the omission of the obligatory redundant characters in the tab and standard notation. The letters (B for Bend, S for Slides, H for Hammer-on, etc.) have been removed in favor of the graphic symbols alone:

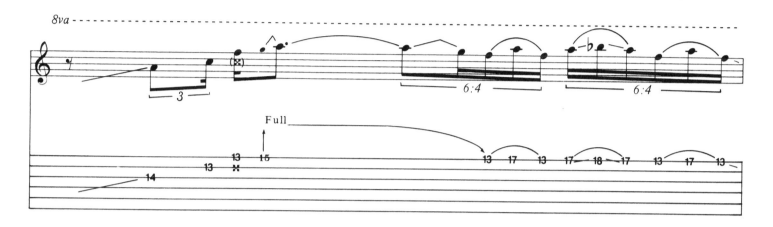

This will yield a two-fold benefit. First, the transcribed score itself will have an uncluttered look which is easier to perceive visually providing a shortcut in the learning process. Second, this format will encourage you, the player, to make the necessary transition from a "tab-only" reader to a guitarist who will begin to relate to standard melodic notation - opening the doors to the worlds of Bach, Paganini, Beethoven, Debussy, Stravinsky and Coltrane. In this format, the laws of common sense will prevail. The following phrase will serve to illustrate the logic of this less cumbersome notation:

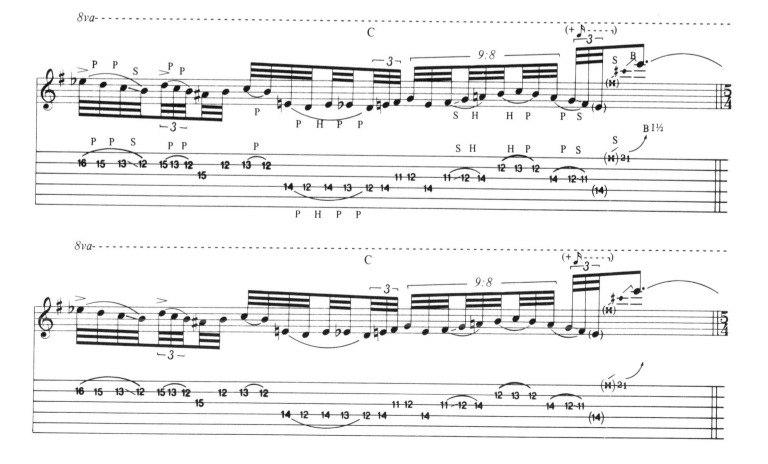

LEGEND

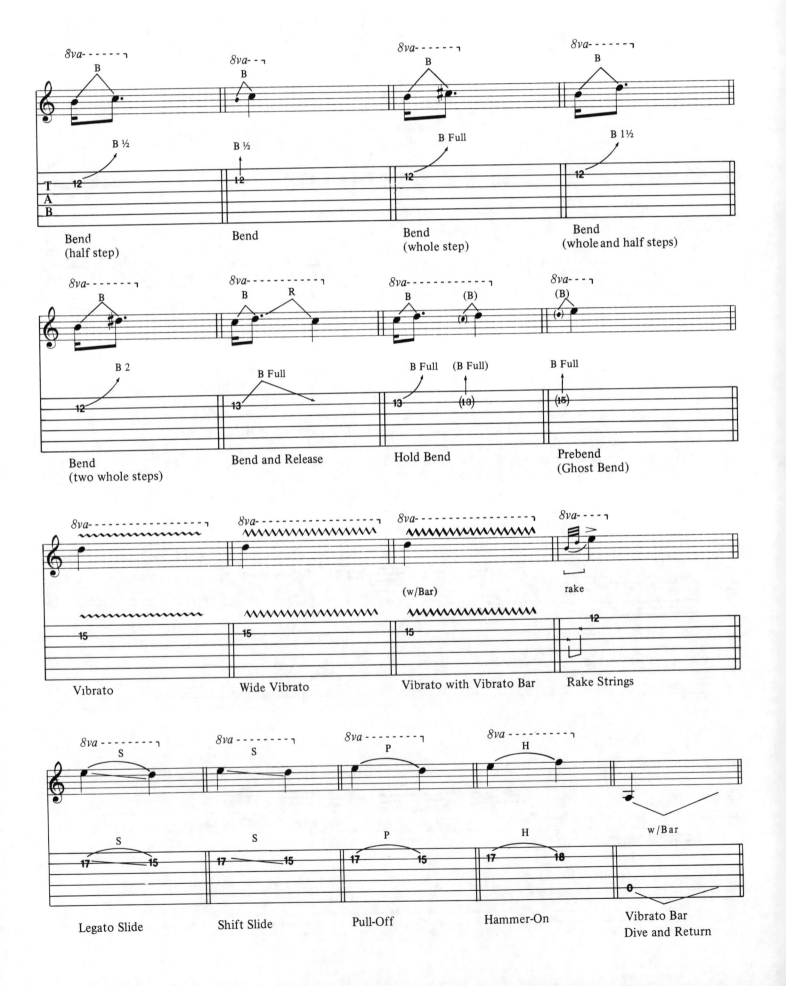

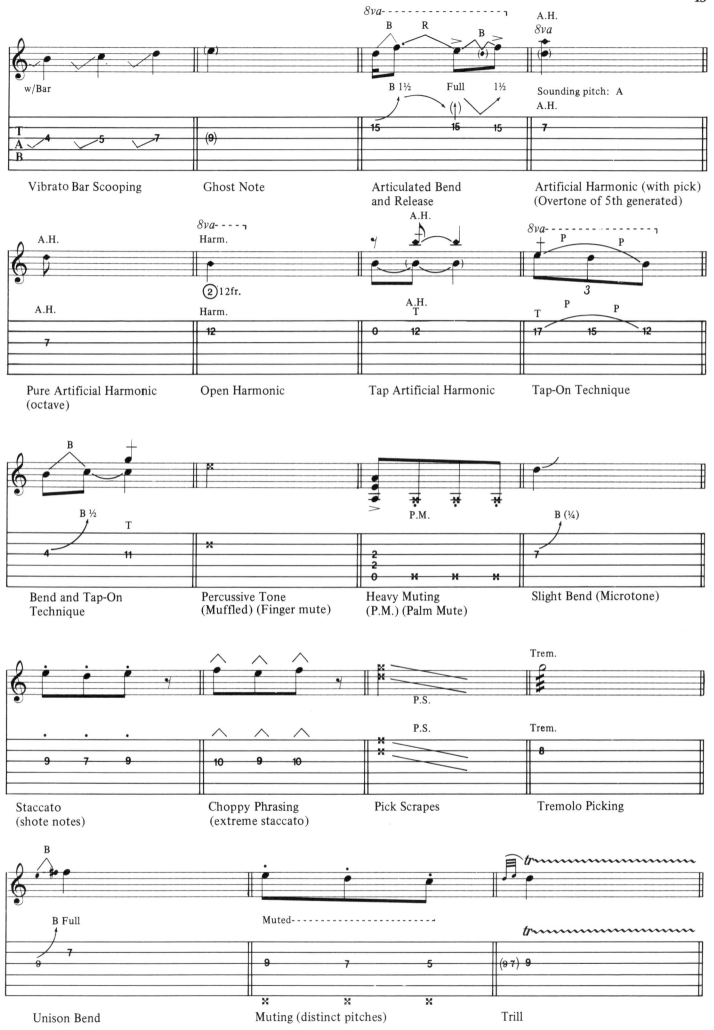

Vibrato Bar Scooping   Ghost Note   Articulated Bend and Release   Artificial Harmonic (with pick) (Overtone of 5th generated)

Pure Artificial Harmonic (octave)   Open Harmonic   Tap Artificial Harmonic   Tap-On Technique

Bend and Tap-On Technique   Percussive Tone (Muffled) (Finger mute)   Heavy Muting (P.M.) (Palm Mute)   Slight Bend (Microtone)

Staccato (shote notes)   Choppy Phrasing (extreme staccato)   Pick Scrapes   Tremolo Picking

Unison Bend   Muting (distinct pitches)   Trill

COMIN' HOME

Words and Music by
BONNIE BRAMLETT and ERIC CLAPTON

We'll soon___ be to - geth - er,___
Got a whole___ lot of lov - in'.___

and that's___ it., I'm com - in' home___ to your___
and ba - by that's why I'm com - in' home___

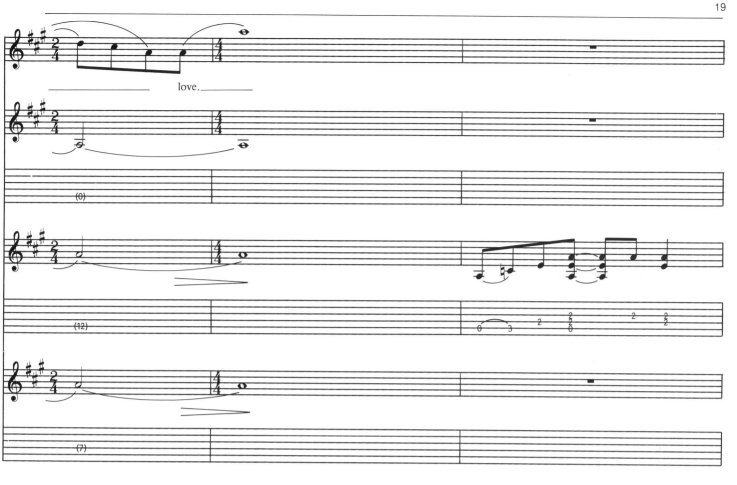

love.

(0)

(12)

(7)

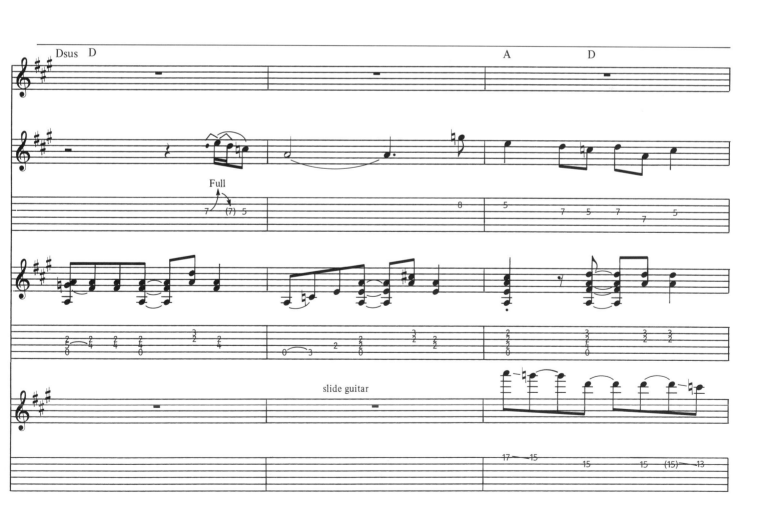

Dsus   D   A   D

Full

slide guitar

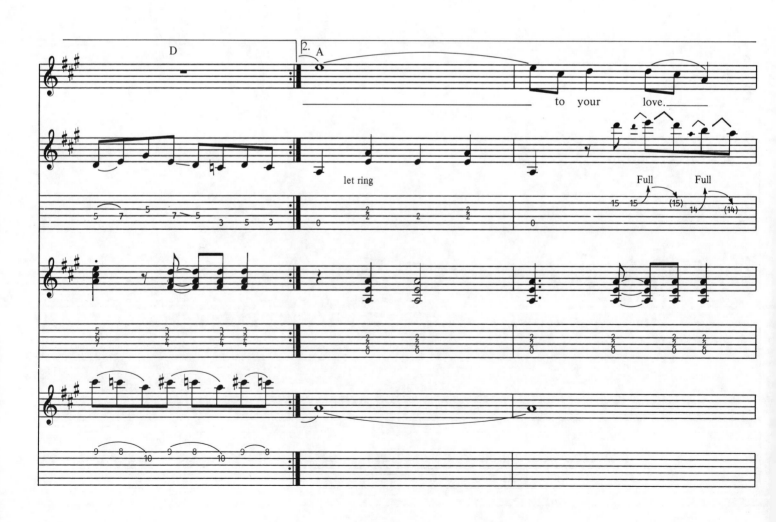

22

Com - in' home._____

D. S. 𝄋 al Coda ⊕

Yeah._____

(slide guitar tacet)

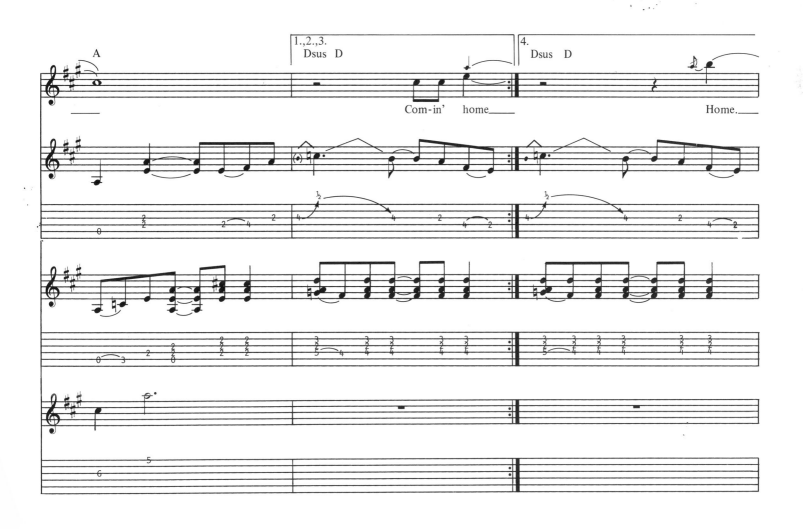

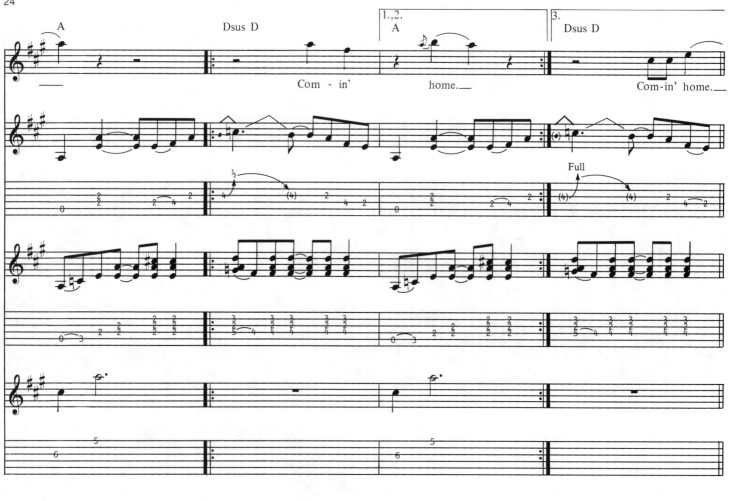

BLUES POWER

Words and Music by
ERIC CLAPTON and LEON RUSSELL

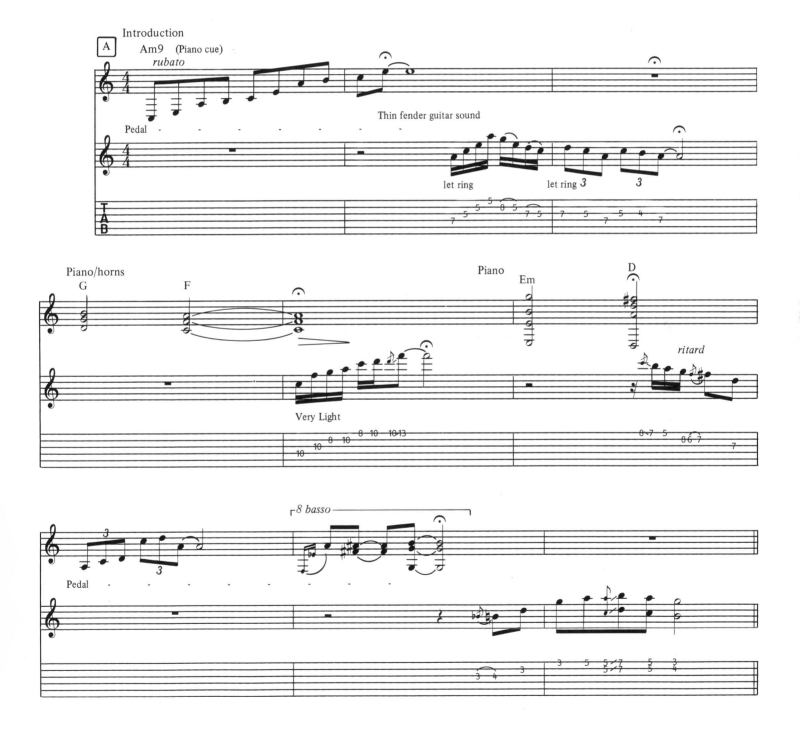

26

There ain't no need for me to be a wall-flow-
There ain't no___ need___ for me to be a wall-flow-

er,___
er,___

'cause now I'm liv-in' on blues___ pow-er.

Guitar Solo Interlude #1

30

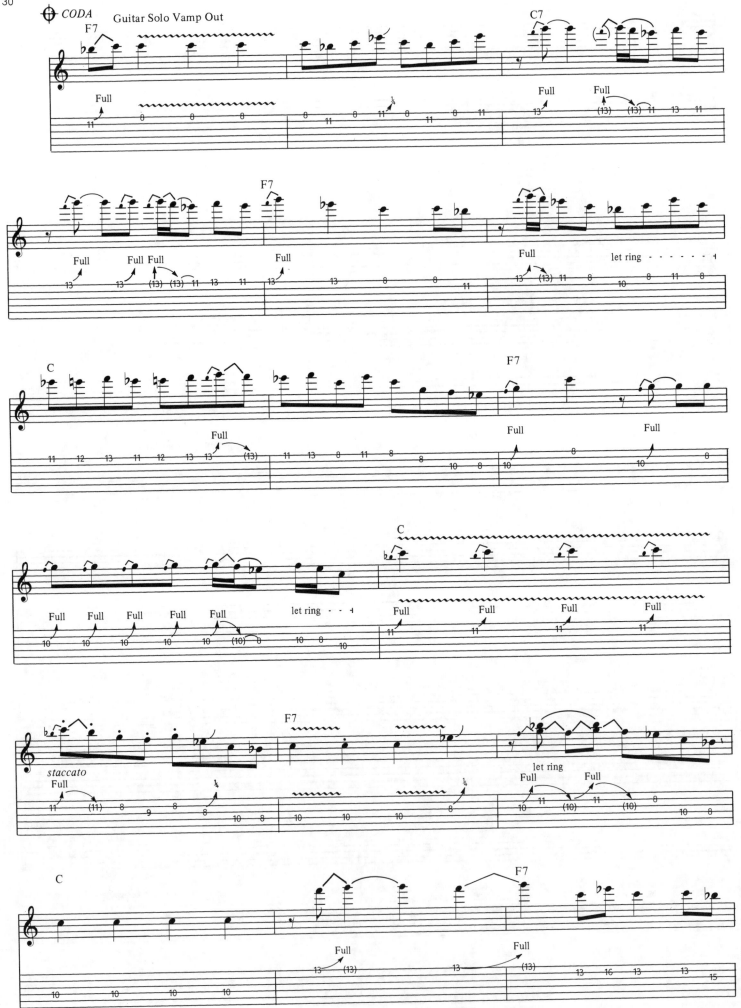

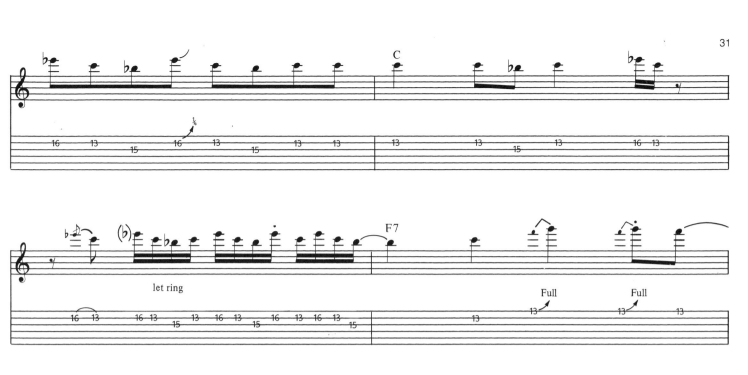

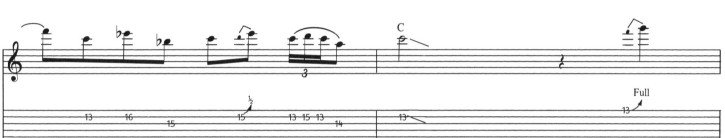

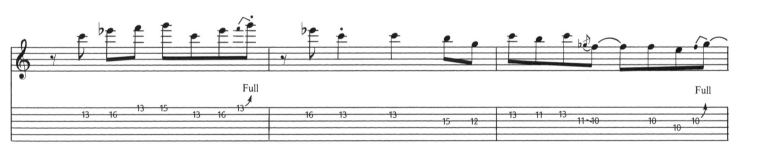

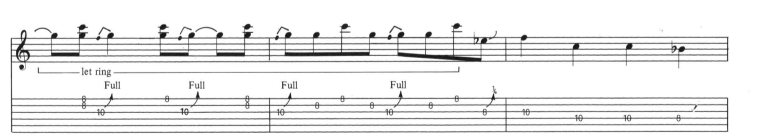

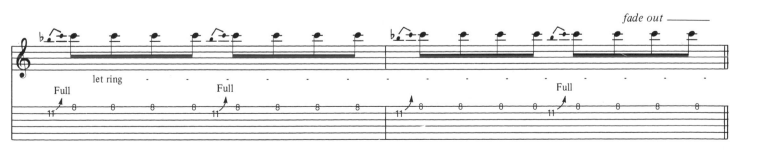

AFTER MIDNIGHT

Words and Music by
JOHN J. CALE

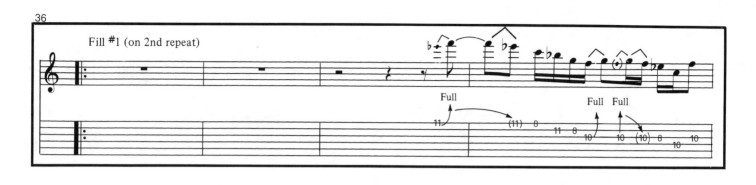

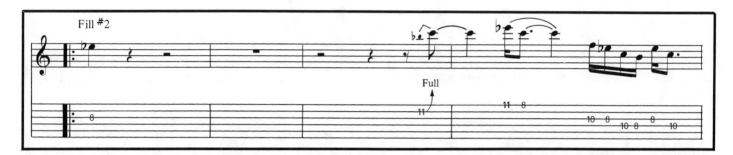

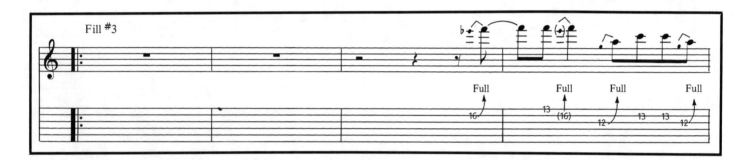

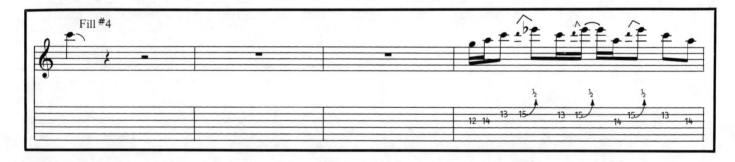

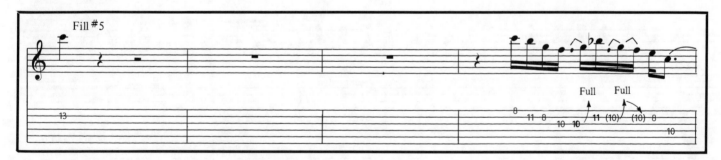

LET IT RAIN

Words and Music by
BONNIE BRAMLETT and ERIC CLAPTON

38

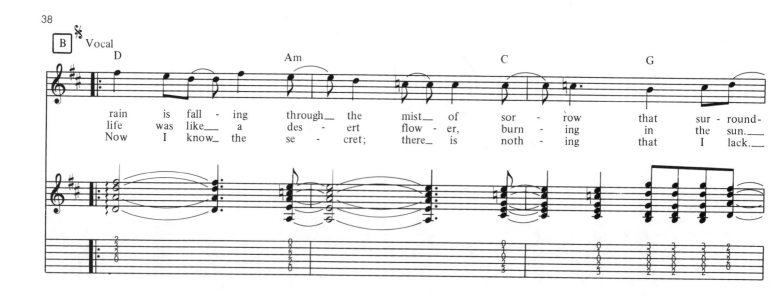

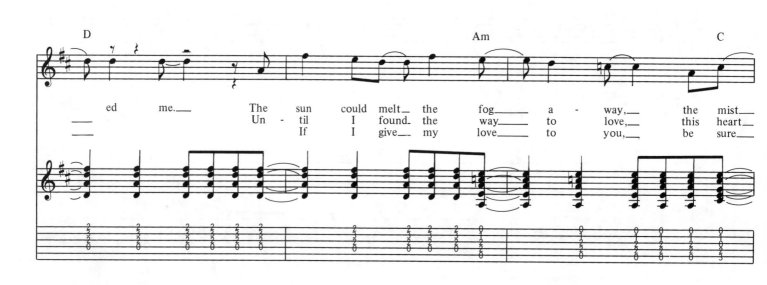

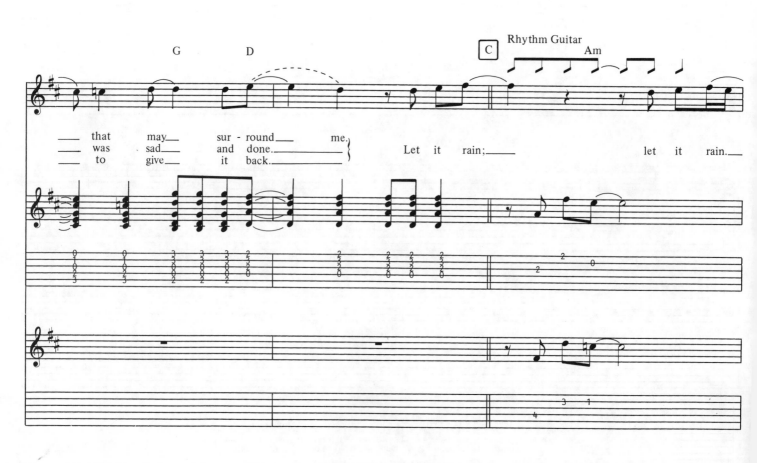

40

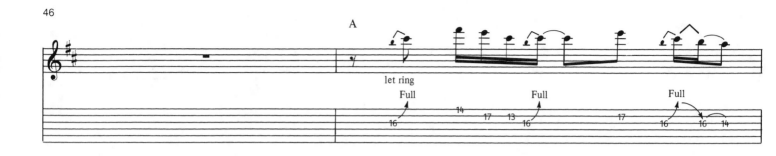

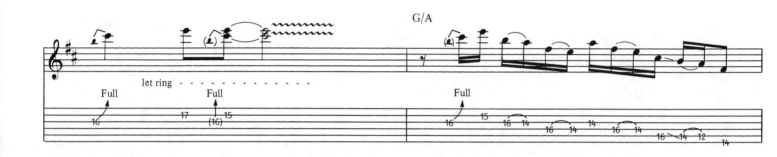

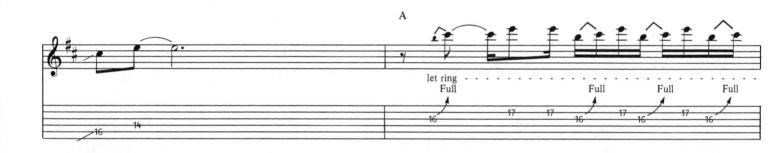

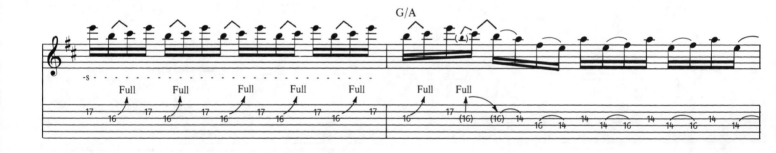

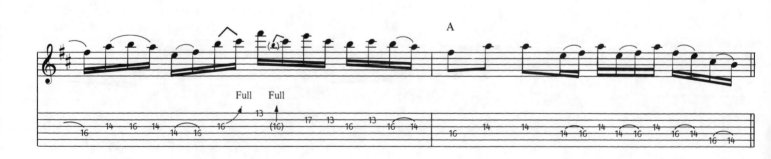

TELL THE TRUTH

Words and Music by
ERIC CLAPTON and BOBBY WHITLOCK

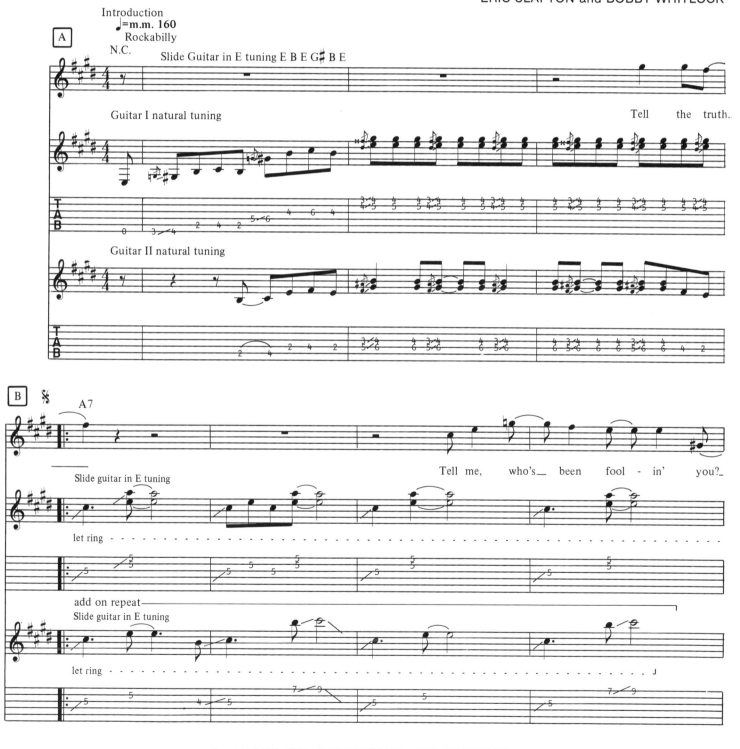

48

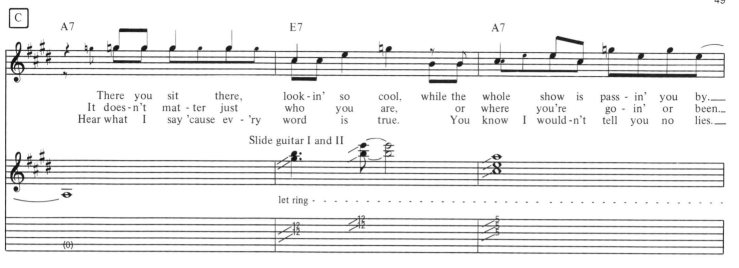

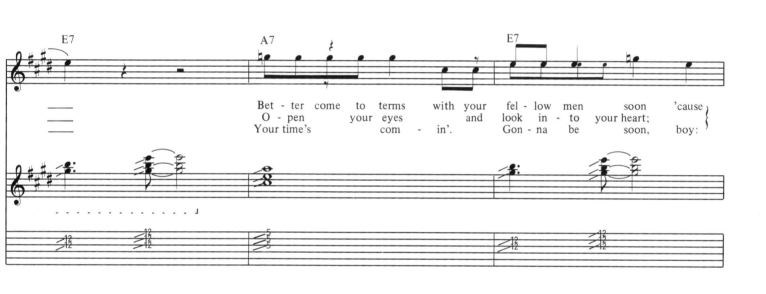

52

it, I can see it. Yeah? I can see it, I can see

it. Yeah! I can see it, I can see it. Yeah!

Instrumental
Slide Guitar Solo #2   Vocal *tacet*   Slide Guitar I

J

let ring - - - - - - - - - - - - - - - - - ♩   tremolo w/pick   long gliss (cont. tremolo)

G   D   E

Slide Guitar II

ROLL IT OVER

Words and Music by
ERIC CLAPTON and BOBBY WHITLOCK

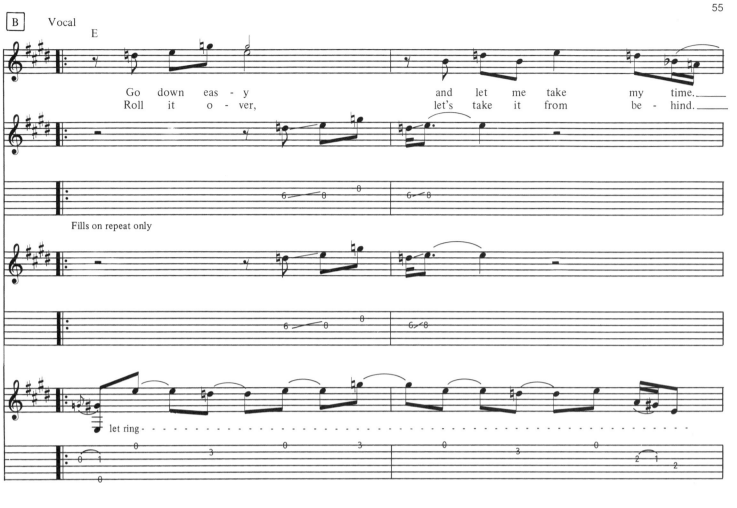

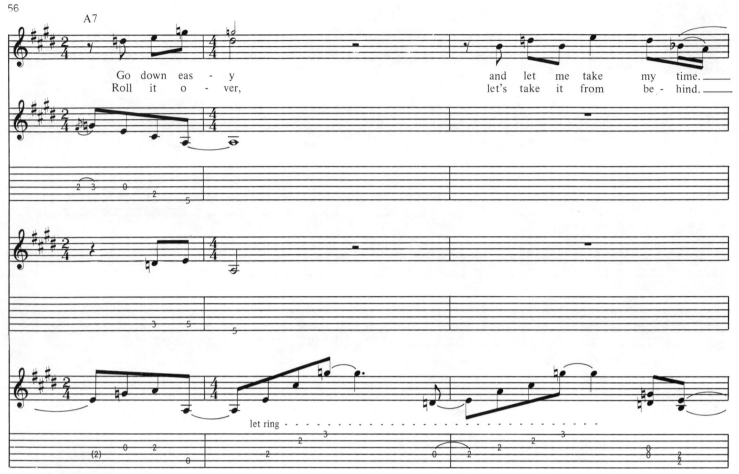

Go down eas - y and let me take my time.____
Roll it o - ver, let's take it from be - hind.____

let ring -

58

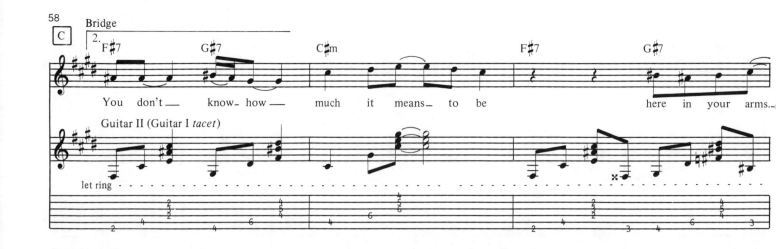

Bridge

2.

You don't know how much it means to be here in your arms.

Guitar II (Guitar I tacet)

let ring - - - - - - -

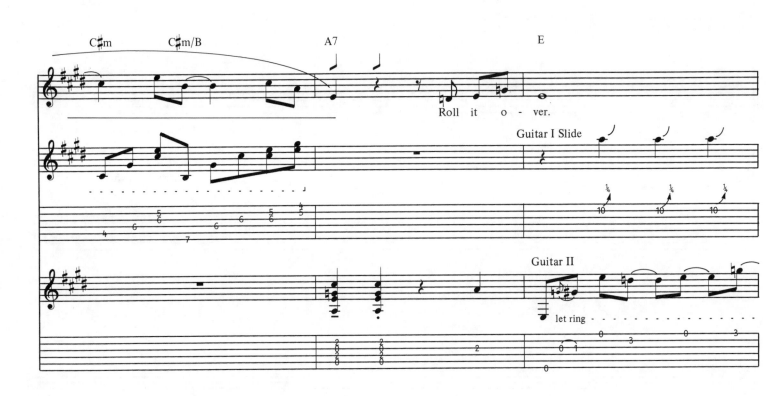

Roll it o - ver.

Guitar I Slide

Guitar II

let ring - - - - - - - - - -

Roll it o - ver

let ring -

D

Go down eas - y and let me take my time.___
Roll it o - ver, let's take it from be - hind.___

Fill on repeat only

A7

Go down eas - y,
Roll it o - ver,
and let me take my time.___
let's take it from be - hind.___

let ring - - - - - - - - - - - - - -

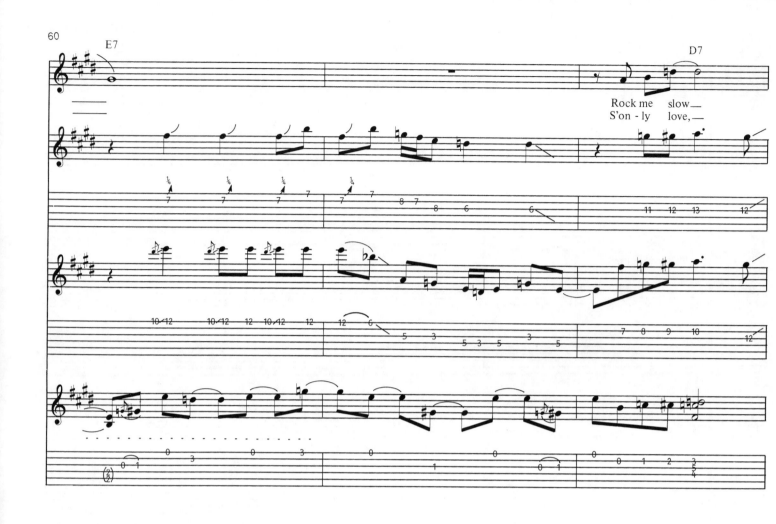

Rock me slow___
S'on - ly love,___

'til I lose my mind._____
God knows it ain't no ___ crime._____

let ring - - - - - - - - - - - - - - - - -

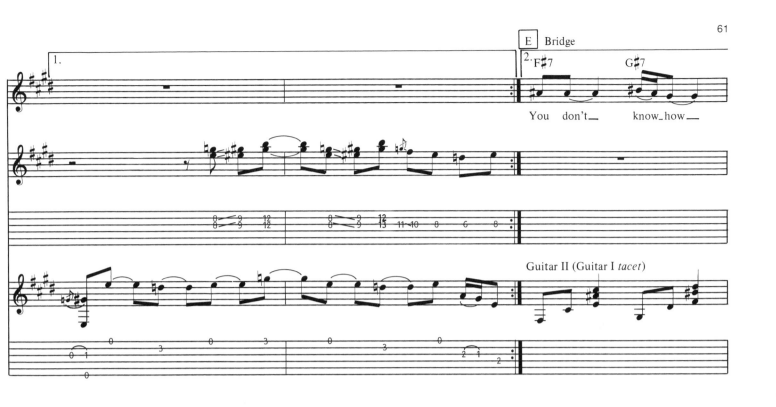

61

Instrumental
Guitar Solo - Wah-Wah/natural tuning

LAYLA

Words and Music by
ERIC CLAPTON and JIM GORDON

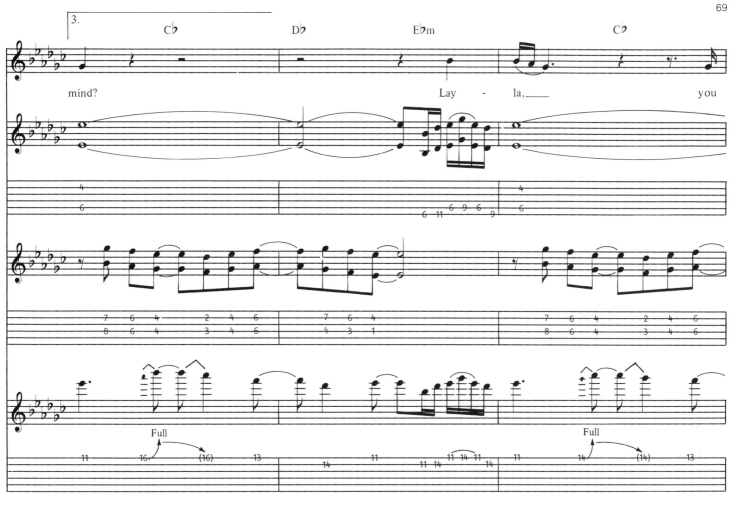

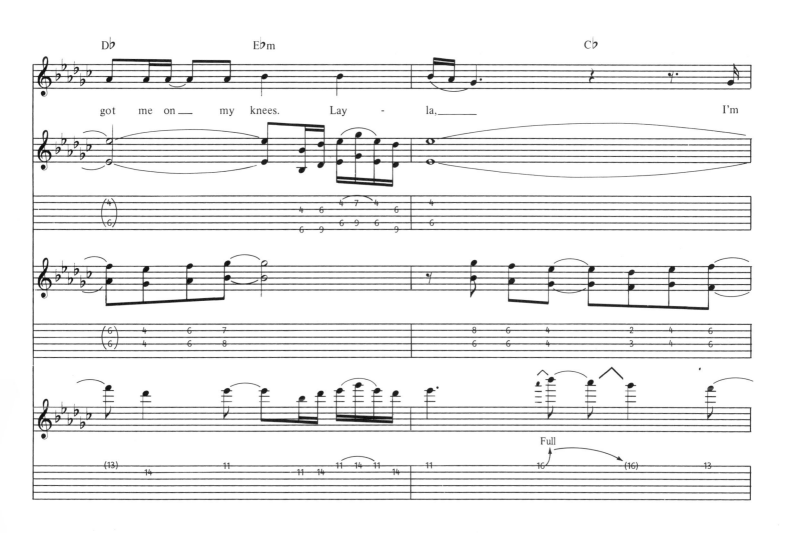

70

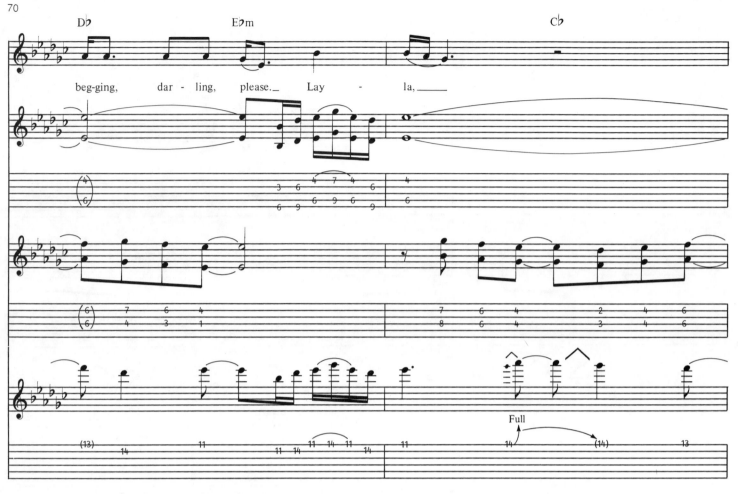

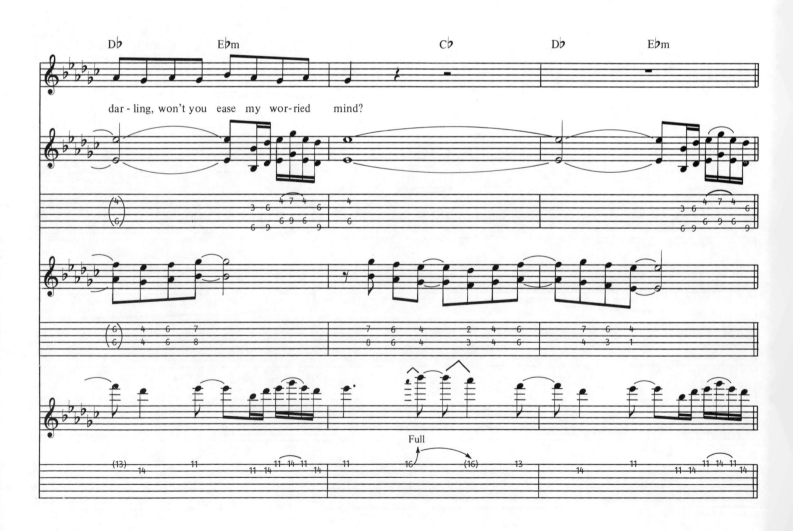

80

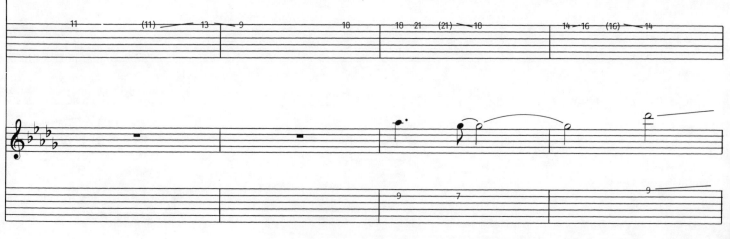

MEAN OLD WORLD

Words and Music by
WALTER JACOBS

This is a mean__ old world, try__ liv-in' by your self.__
I've got the blues,____ I'll pack my things and go.__

slap strings on frets

Can't get the ones you're lov-in',
I guess you don't love me,

no slide ————————————— slide in

have to use some-bod-y else.__
luck-y Mis-ter So and So,__

Instrumental
Guitar Solo #1

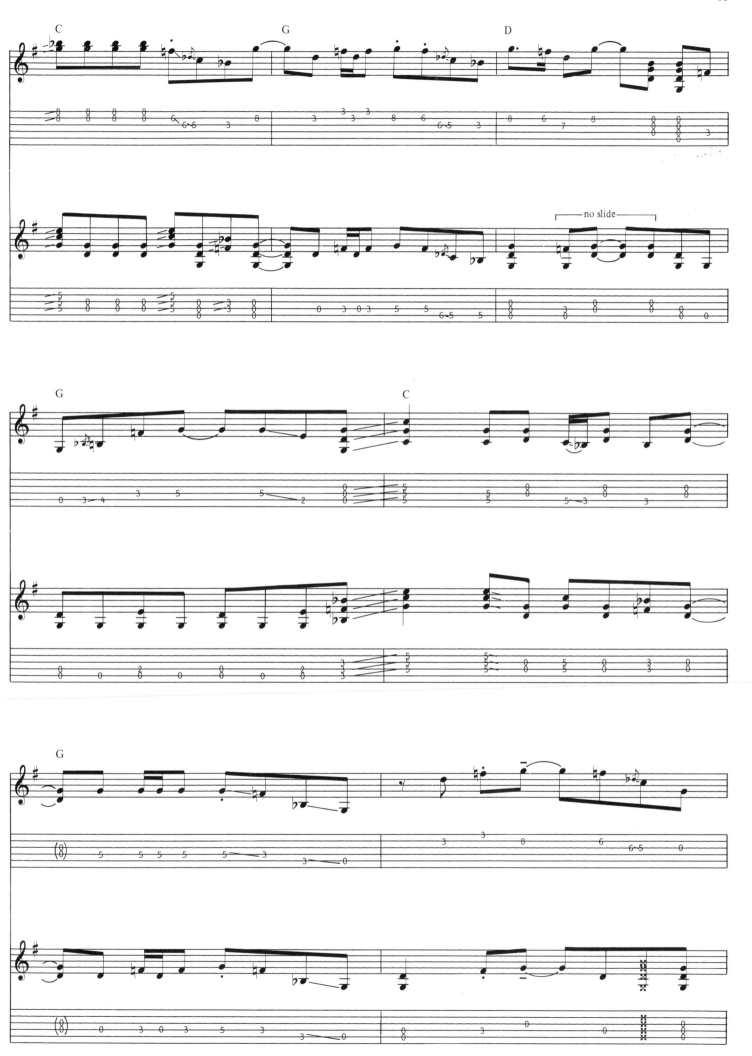

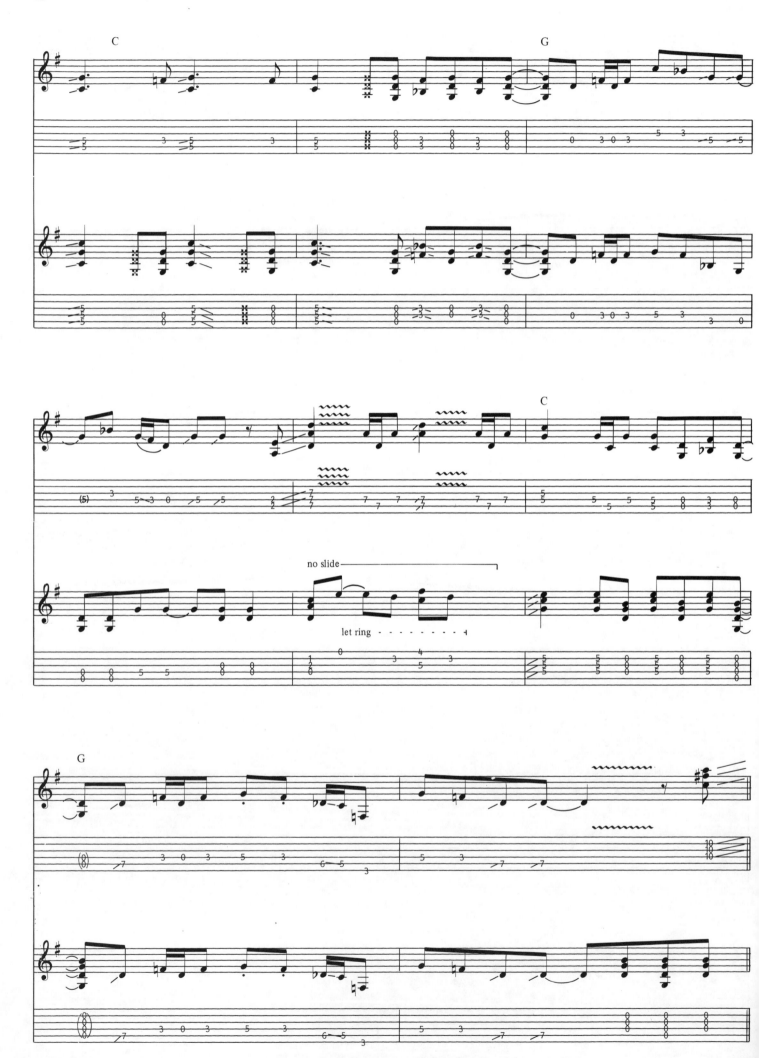

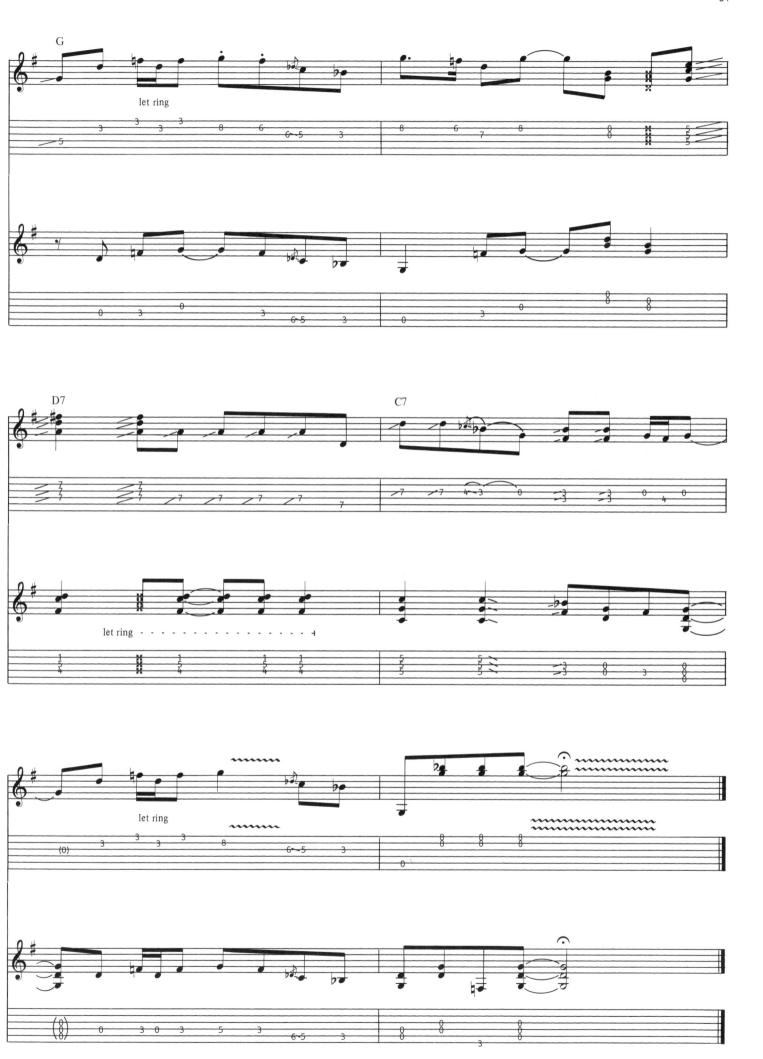

KEY TO THE HIGHWAY

Words and Music by
BIG BILL BROONZY and CHAS. SEGAR

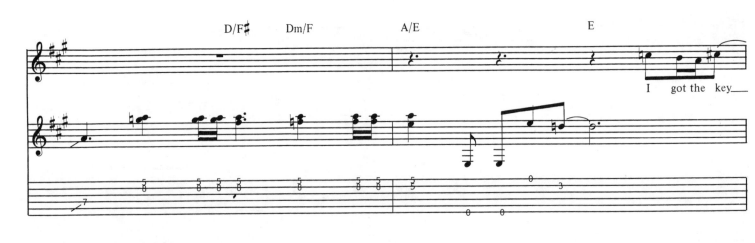

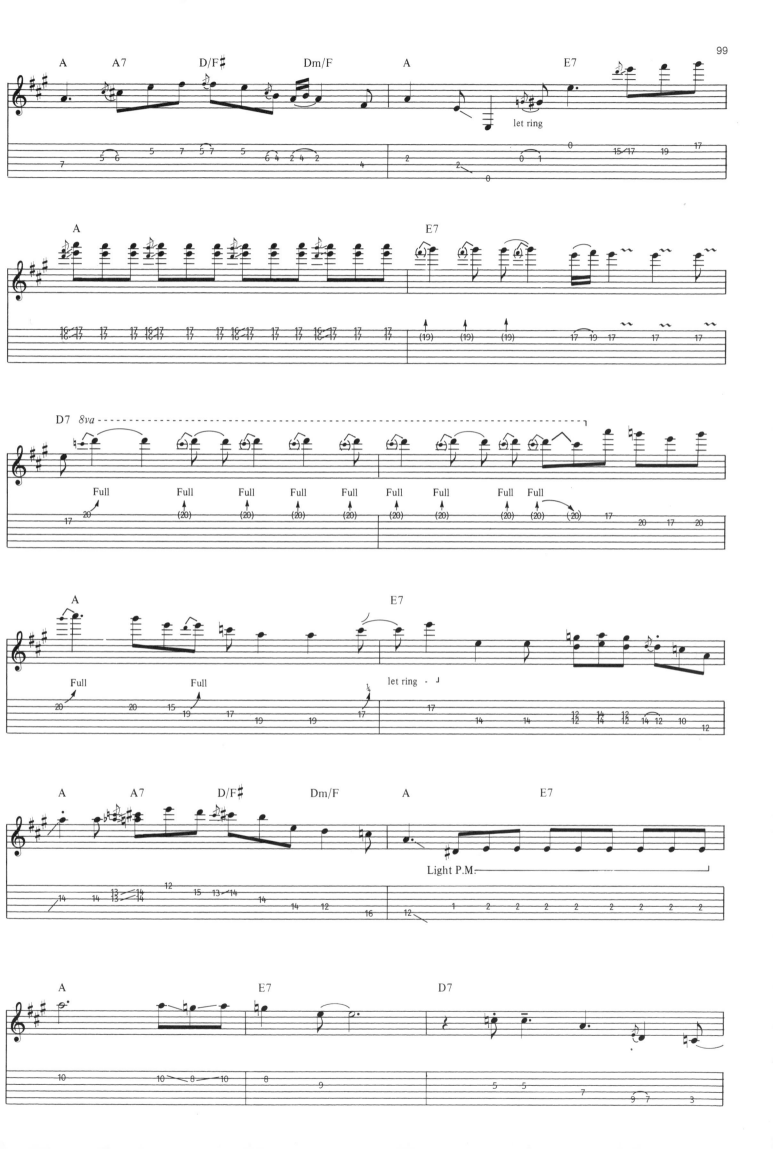

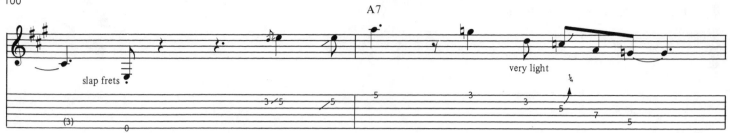

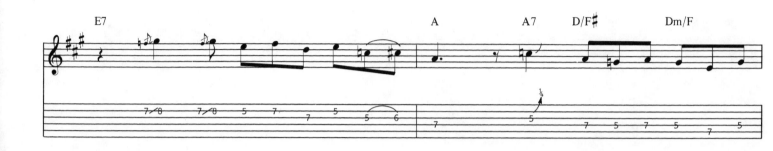

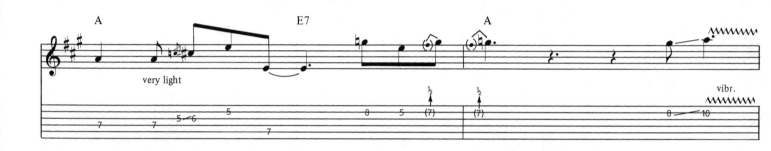

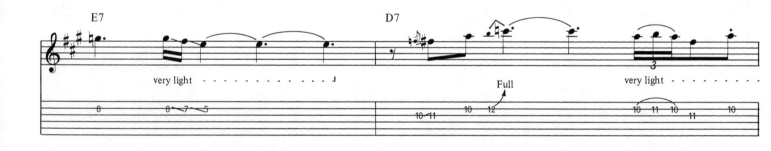

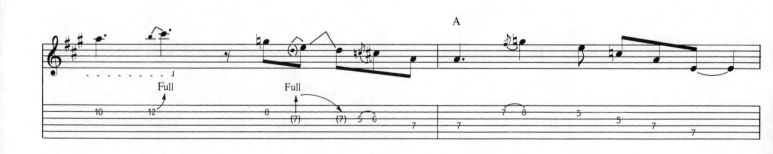

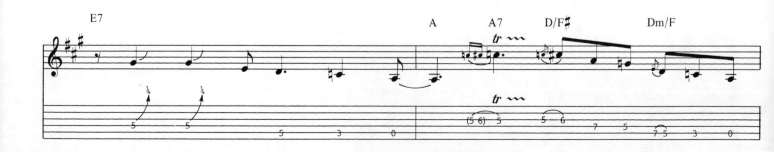

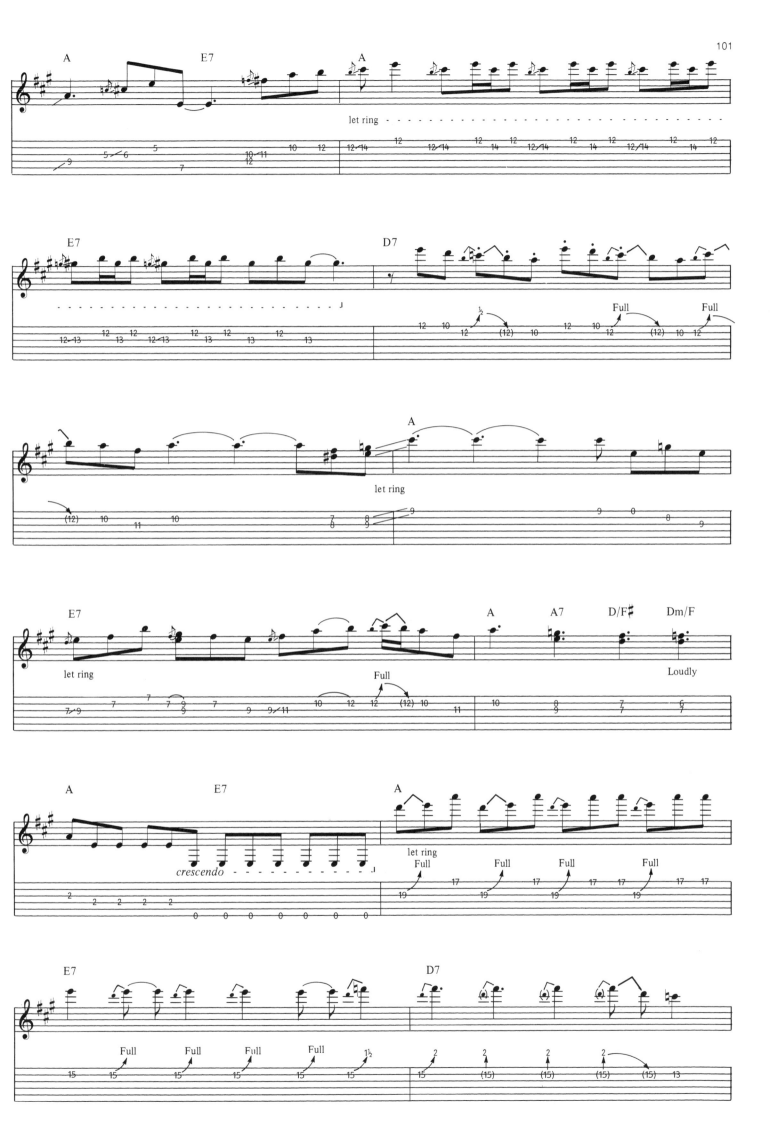

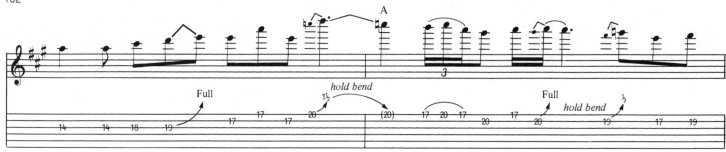

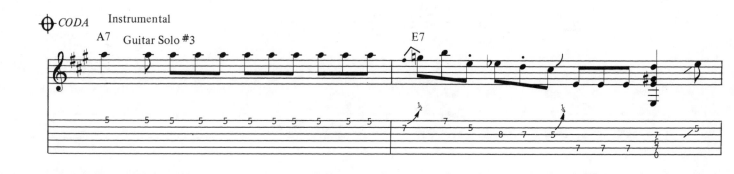

CROSSROADS

Words and Music by
ERIC CLAPTON

105

106

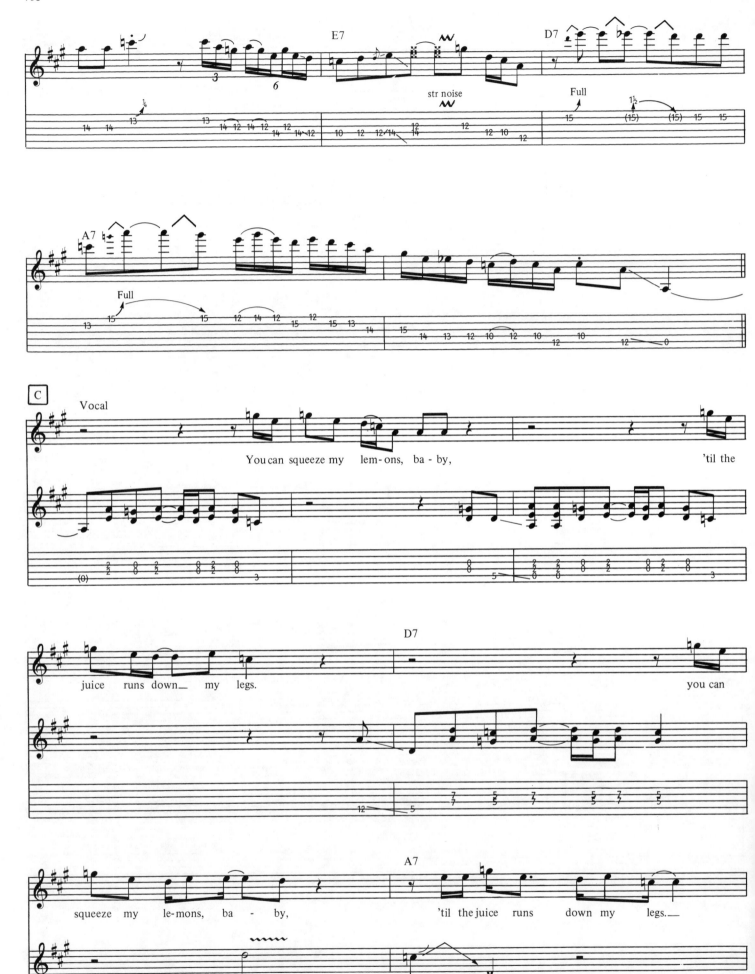

*lyrics are not clear on this line, so they are not necessarily what are sung.

D Instrumental - Guitar Solo

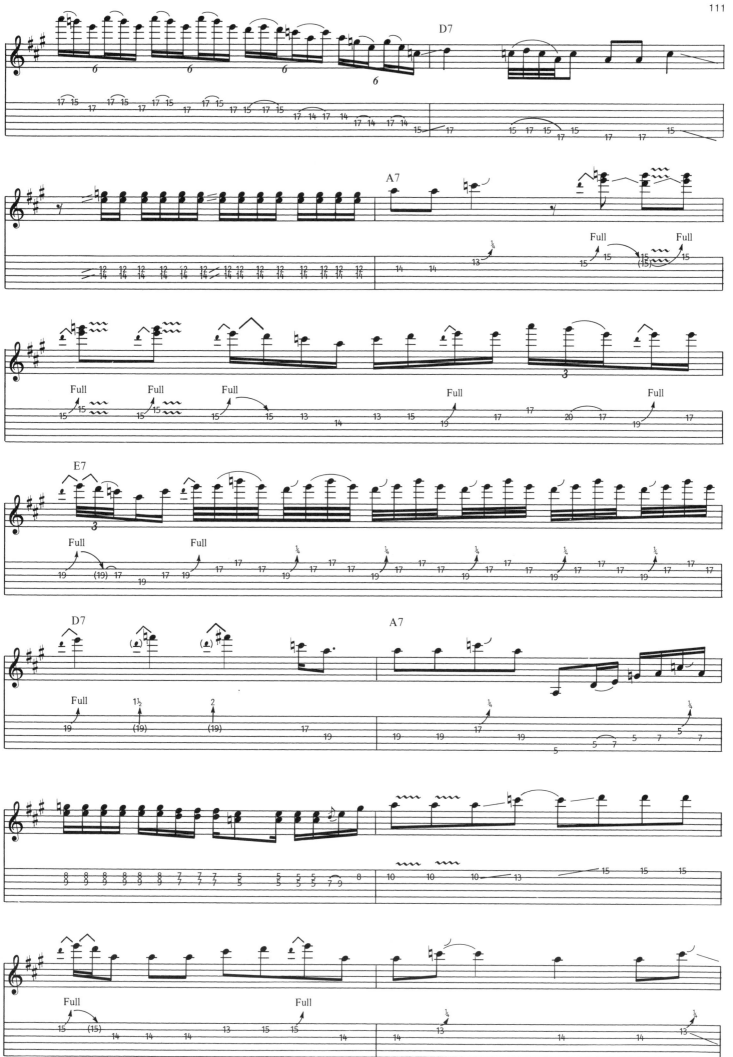

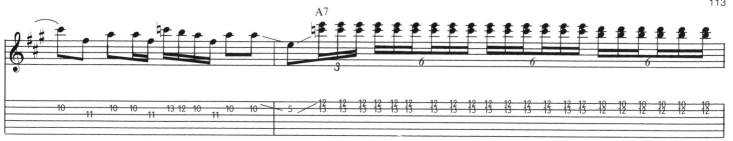

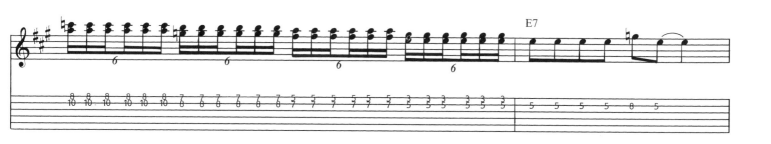

CADENZA

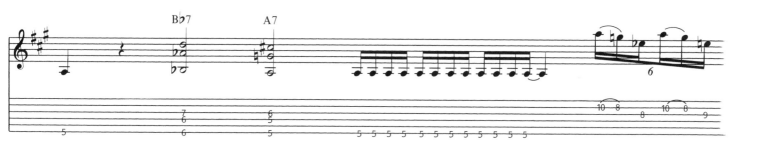

GOT TO GET BETTER IN A LITTLE WHILE

Words and Music by
ERIC CLAPTON

Continue "Rhythm Figure 1"
Guitar I/Wah-Wah

A Vocal

"Rhythm Figure 1"

Don't you know___ what's wrong with me?___
Rev - o - lu - tion all a - cross___ the land.

let ring -

Fills on repeat

I'm see - in'___ things I don't want to see.___
Just like Sly you've got ___ to ___ make a stand.

"Rhythm Figure 1"

Sip - pin'___ things___ that ain't
Please don't hurt no - bod-y, don't_

116

Guitar Solo

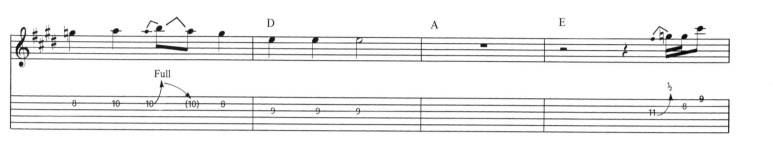
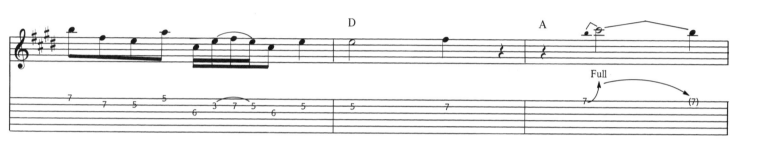
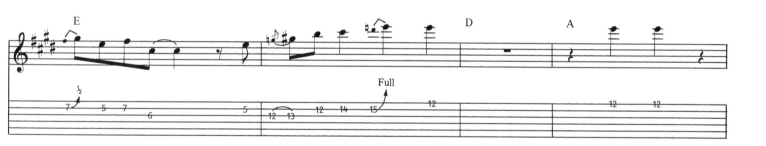
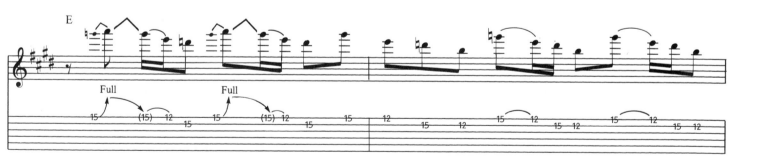
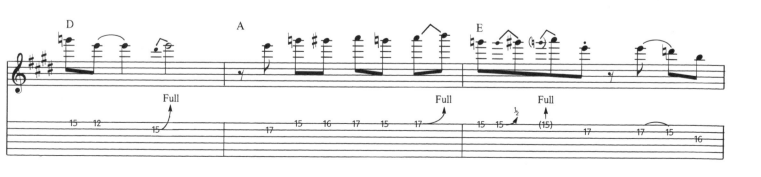

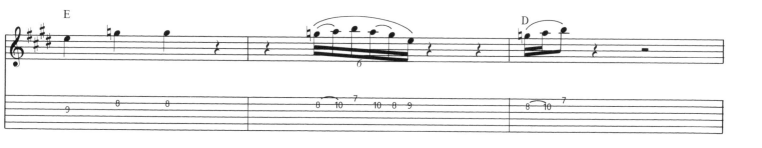

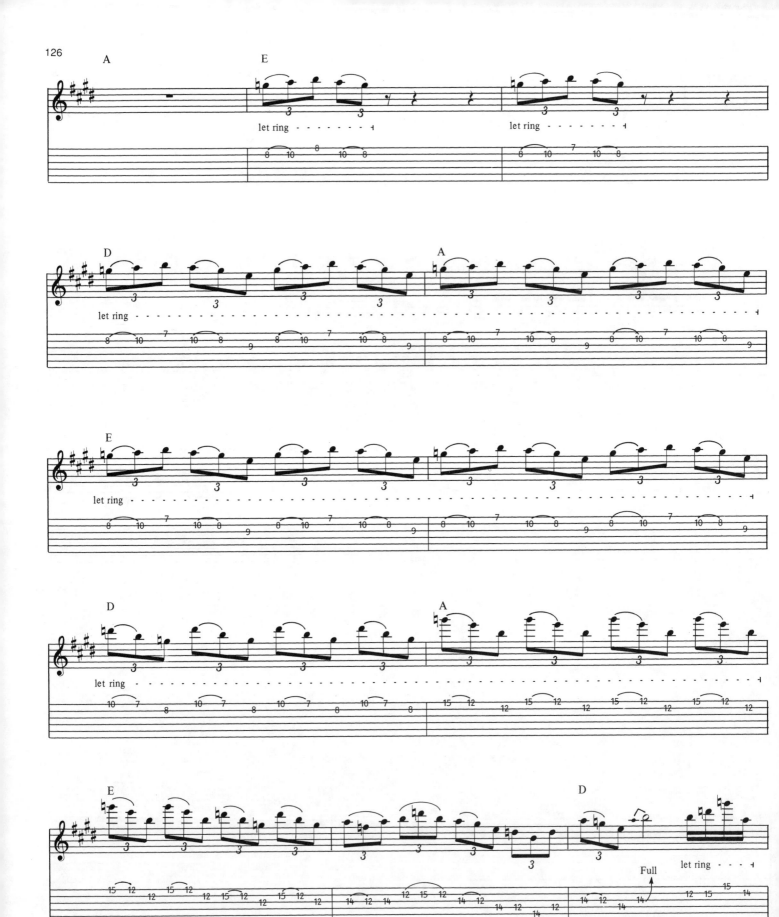

EVIL

Words and Music by
WILLIE DIXON

Vocal

It's a long
You make it_____

Guitar II Fills

Guitar II Fills on repeat only

way from home._____
to your house,

130

Can't sleep at night.
knock on the front door.

Call on your tel - e - phone;
Run 'round to the back;

Some - thin' just _____ ain't_right.
You catch him_ just_ be - fore he goes.

That's e - vil,

Cue notes on D.S.

e - vil___ is go - in' on wrong.

I have___ warned you broth - er,___   I'm gon - na warn you broth - er,___

(1. 2.) you bet - ter watch your hap - py home.
(3.) you bet - ter watch your hap - py___

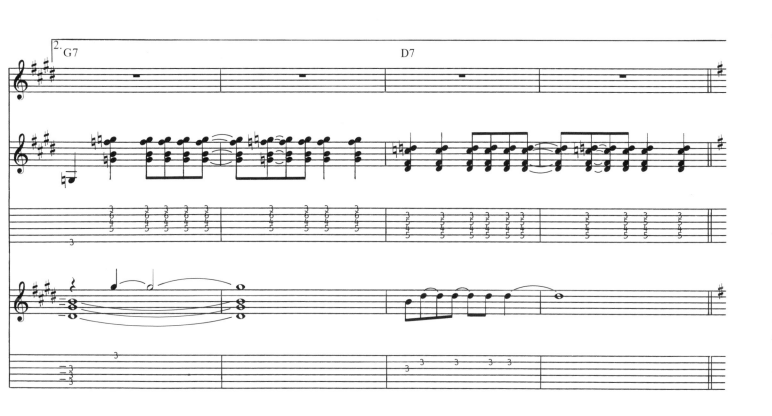

B Instrumental

G7   Double Guitar Solo

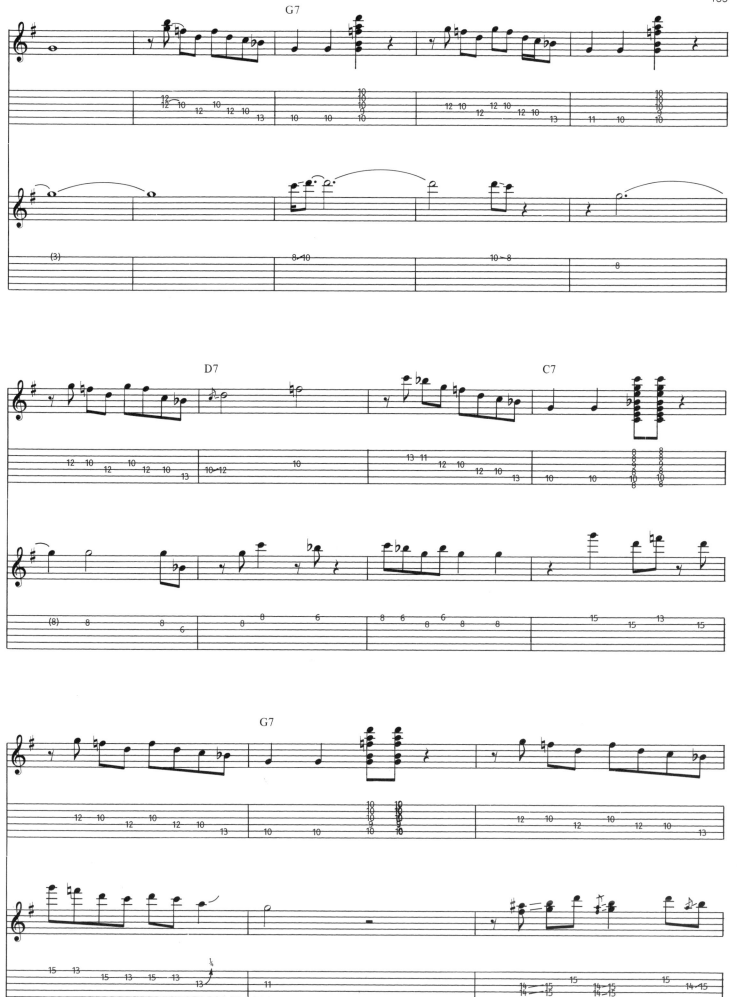

136

Eighth note pick strokes on gliss

138

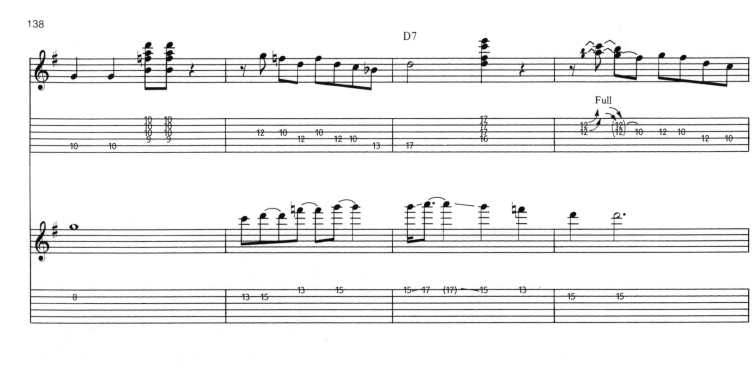

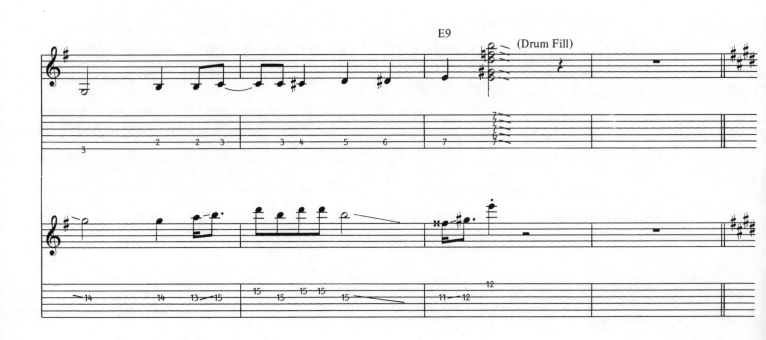

Grab the first____ thing__ smok - in';

an' you__ have - ta hol - ler__

D. S. 𝄋 al Coda ⊕

__ go____ home.

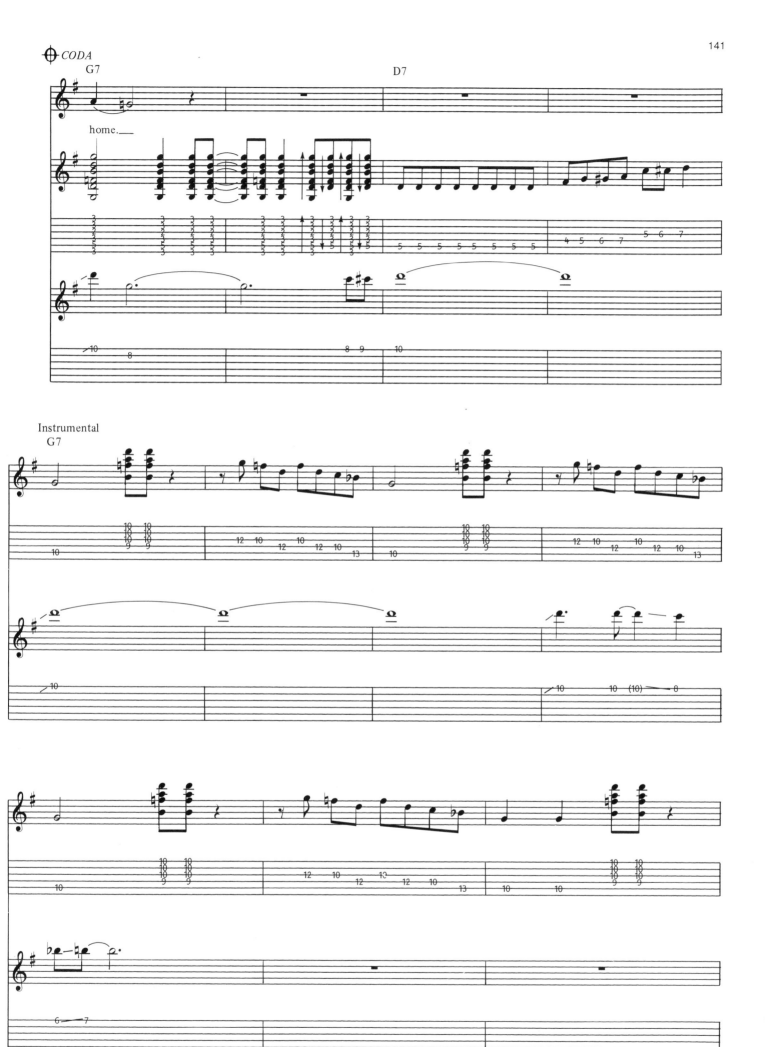

ONE MORE CHANCE

Words and Music by
ERIC CLAPTON

148

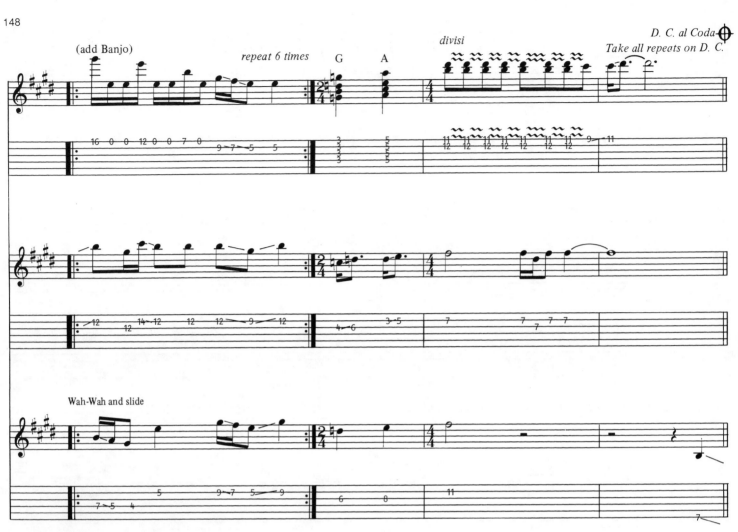

give me one more chance.

Won't you give me one more chance.

MEAN OLD FRISCO

Words and Music by
ARTHUR CRUDUP

MCA MUSIC PUBLISHING

150

SNAKE LAKE BLUES

Words and Music by
ERIC CLAPTON and BOBBY WHITLOCK

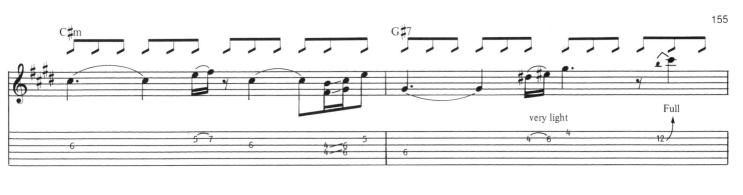

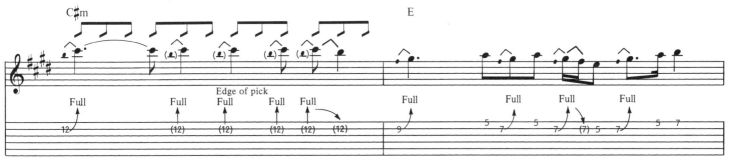

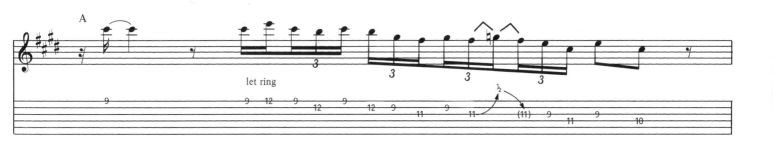

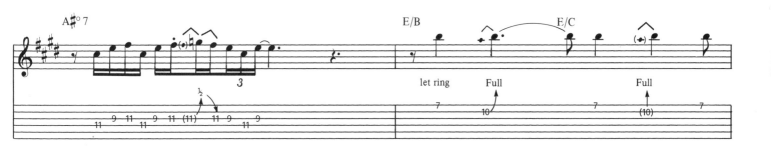

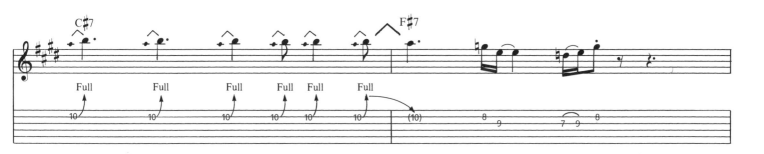

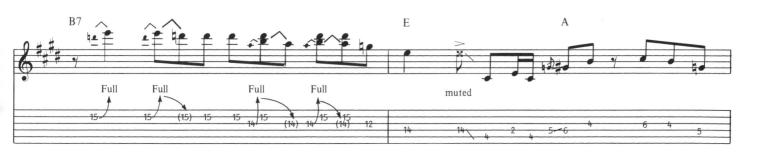

LET IT GROW

Words and Music by
ERIC CLAPTON

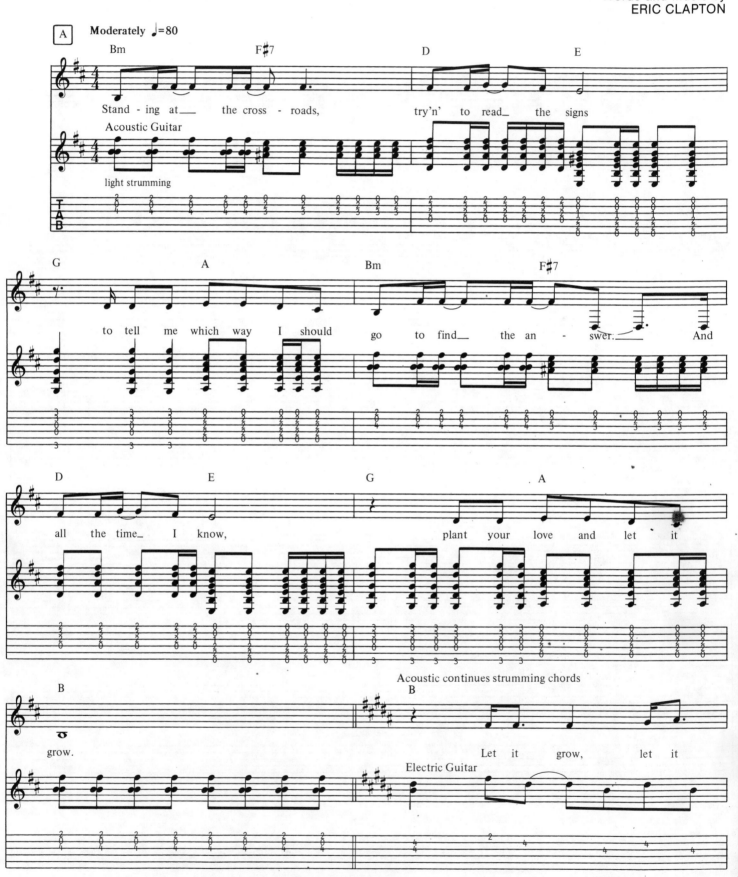

AIN'T THAT LOVIN' YOU

Words and Music by
JIMMY REED

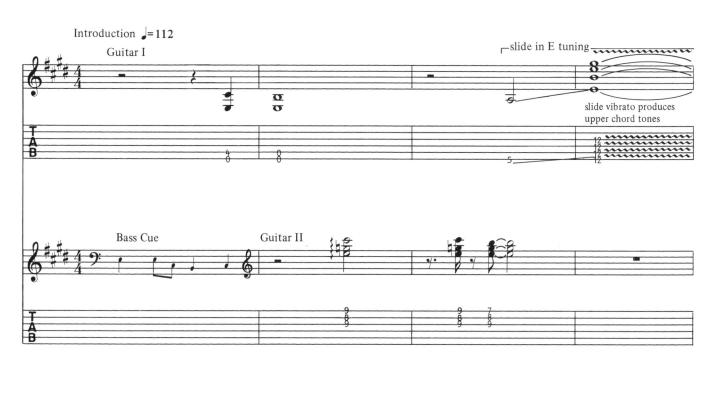

You don't know me, ba - by, like I know my - self.___
Let me tell you some - thing, I swear to God it's true.___

I just want to love___ you,___ ba - by, but you
If you give your love___ to me,___ I'm

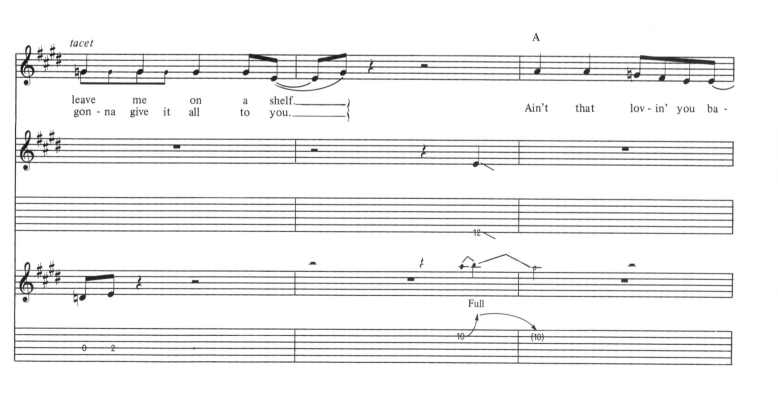

leave me on a shelf.___
gon - na give it all to you.___

Ain't that lov - in' you ba -

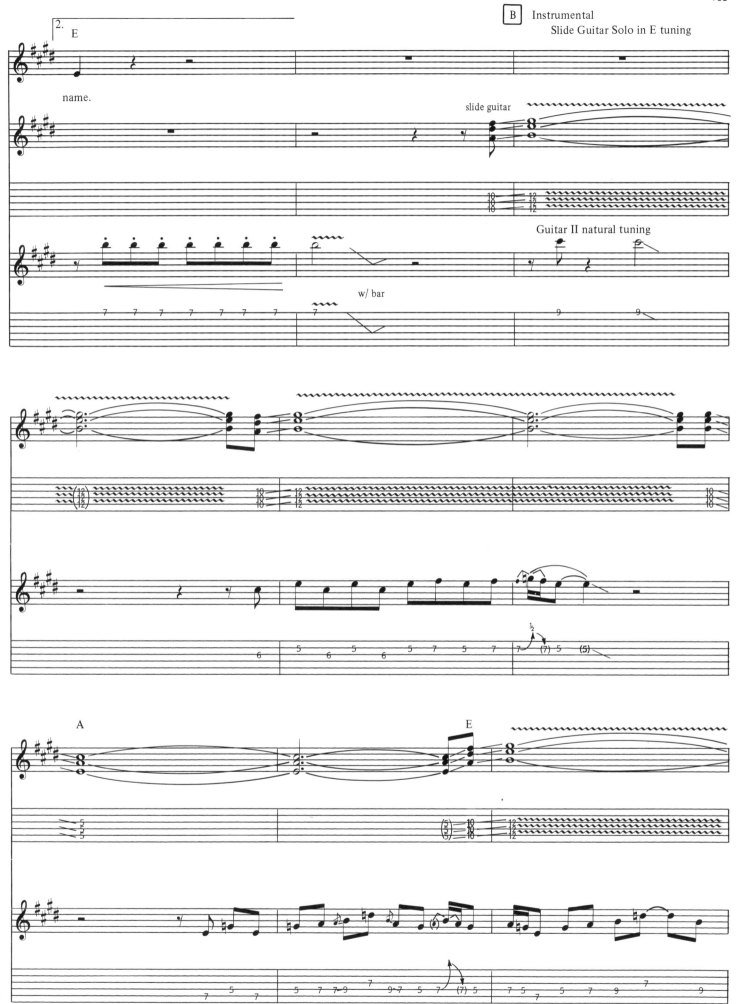

B Instrumental
Slide Guitar Solo in E tuning

172

*lyrics are not clear on this line, so they are not necessarily what are sung.

174

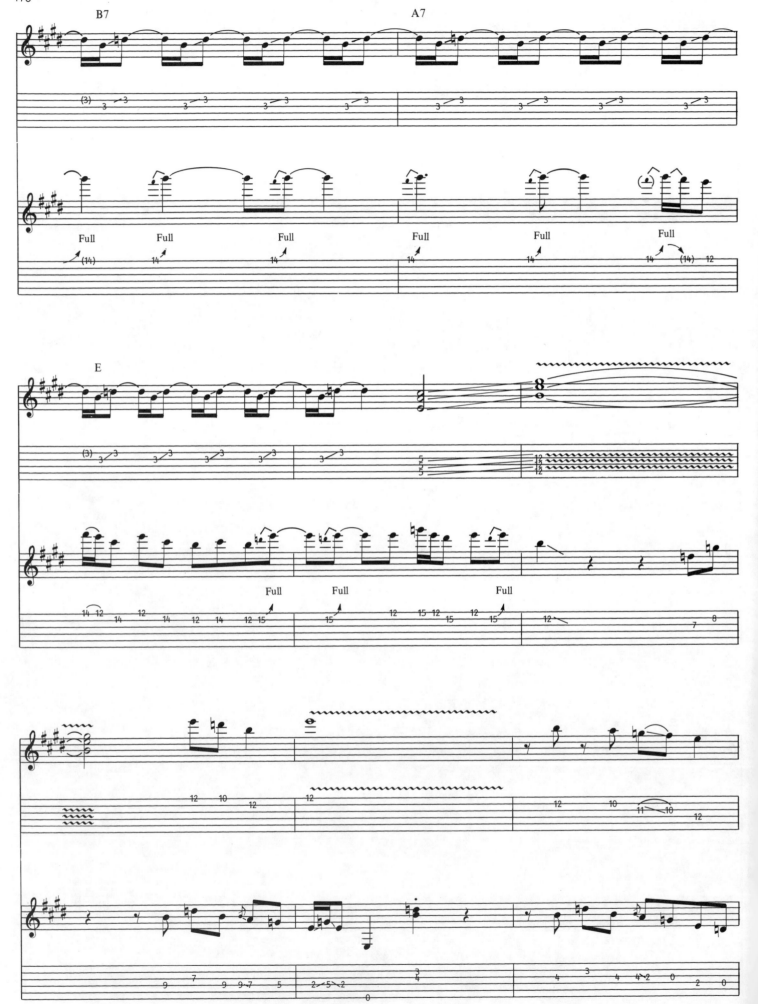

MOTHERLESS CHILDREN

Arranged by
ERIC CLAPTON and CARL RADLE

182

186

I SHOT THE SHERIFF

Words and Music by
BOB MARLEY

192

200

BETTER MAKE IT THROUGH TODAY

Words and Music by
ERIC CLAPTON

205

Recorded Versions are terrific note-for-note guitar transcriptions of the hottest and biggest names in music — today and yesterday. Each Recorded Versions arrangement is accurately transcribed into standard notation and tablature so you can play the music of these artists exactly as they recorded it! Note-for-note, the hottest guitar product you can buy!

THE BEST OF AEROSMITH
15 of their greatest. 00692015 $16.95

THE BEST OF GEORGE BENSON
14 of his best. 00699041 $12.95

CHUCK BERRY
Includes: Back In The U.S.A. • Guitar Boogie • Johnny B. Goode • Mabellene • Roll Over Beethoven • more.
00692385 $14.95

CINDERELLA — LONG COLD WINTER
Matching folio to their most recent album.
00692376 $16.95

CINDERELLA — NIGHT SONGS
Matching folio to the hit album. 00692375 $14.95

THE BEST OF ERIC CLAPTON
12 of his best. 00692391 $14.95

ERIC CLAPTON — CROSSROADS VOL. 1
30 songs from the first volume of this collector's edition LP.
00692392 $16.95

ERIC CLAPTON — CROSSROADS VOL. 2
20 songs from the second volume of this collector's edition LP.
00692393 $16.95

ERIC CLAPTON — CROSSROADS VOL. 3
23 songs from the third volume of this collector's edition LP.
00692394 $16.95

DEF LEPPARD — HYSTERIA
Matching folio to the LP. 00692430 $16.95

BO DIDDLEY GUITAR SOLOS
Songs include: Bo Diddley • Diddy Wah Diddy • Hey! Bo Diddley • I'm A Man • Mona (I Need You Baby).
00692240 $14.95

GREAT ROCKABILLY GUITAR SOLOS
18 songs including: Blue Suede Shoes • Hound Dog • Peggy Sue • Hello Mary Lou • Stray Cat Strut • Highway 40 Blues • and more!
00692820 $14.95

HEAVY METAL BASS LICKS — I
18 songs by Yngwie Malmsteen, Judas Priest, Def Leppard, Poison, Ratt, and Cinderella 00692878 $16.95

HEAVY METAL BASS LICKS — II
18 songs by Ratt, Def Leppard, Yngwie Malmsteen, Iron Maiden, Judas Priest, Poison and Cinderella 00692879 $16.95

JIMI HENDRIX — ARE YOU EXPERIENCED?
11 songs from the LP. 00692930 $19.95

JIMI HENDRIX — AXIS: BOLD AS LOVE
13 songs from the LP. 00692931 $19.95

JIMI HENDRIX — ELECTRIC LADYLAND
16 songs from the LP. 00692932 $22.95

INXS
10 of their best. 00693085 $14.95

IRON MAIDEN
Guitar transcriptions to all of the songs from their first four albums: Killers; Iron Maiden; The Number Of The Beast; Peace Of Mind.
00693095 $19.95

IRON MAIDEN — POWERSLAVE/SOMEWHERE IN TIME
Matching folio to the albums ''Powerslave'' and ''Somewhere In Time.'' 00693096 $17.95

IRON MAIDEN — SEVENTH SON OF A SEVENTH SON
Matching folio to their most recent album.
00693097 $16.95

JUDAS PRIEST — VOLUME I
15 of their best. 00693185 $16.95

JUDAS PRIEST — VOLUME II
13 more hits. 00693186 $16.95

JUDAS PRIEST CLASSICS
12 songs from this heavy metal group. 00693188 $16.95

JUDAS PRIEST — RAM IT DOWN
10 songs from the album. 00693187 $16.95

LYNYRD SKYNYRD
A collection of their best. 00693412 $14.95

YNGWIE MALMSTEEN — MARCHING OUT
Matching folio to the LP. 00694756 $14.95

YNGWIE MALMSTEEN — RISING FORCE
Matching folio to the smash LP. 00694755 $16.95

YNGWIE MALMSTEEN — TRILOGY
Matching folio to the LP. 00694757 $16.95

MASTERS OF ROCK
22 songs including: Boys Are Back In Town • Foxy Lady • Layla • Livin' On A Prayer. 00693474 $16.95

METAL MADNESS
16 classic metal tunes, including: Dance • Heaven Tonight • I'm A Rocker.
00692880 $16.95

NIGHT RANGER — 7 WISHES
Matching folio to the hit album. 00693632 $9.95

PINK FLOYD EARLY CLASSICS
13 of their greatest hits. 00693800 $14.95

POISON — LOOK WHAT THE CAT DRAGGED IN
Matching folio to the LP: 00693865 $14.95

POISON — OPEN UP & SAY AHH
10 songs from the album. 00693866 $16.95

THE BEST OF POLICE
19 of their best 00693864 $14.95

ELVIS PRESLEY
18 songs including: Heartbreak Hotel • Blue Suede Shoes • Hound Dog • Jailhouse Rock 00692535 $14.95

RATT — DANCING UNDERCOVER
Matching folio to the LP: 00693912 $16.95

RATT — INVASION OF YOUR PRIVACY
Matching folio to the hit album. 00693910 $12.95

RATT — OUT OT THE CELLAR
Matching folio to the smash LP: 00693911 $16.95

STRYPER — IN GOD WE TRUST
10 songs from the album of the same name. 00694180 $16.95

THE BEST OF U2
10 of their best. 00694410 $16.95

U2 — THE JOSHUA TREE
Matching folio to the critically acclaimed smash LP.
00694411 $14.95

THE FRANK ZAPPA GUITAR BOOK
22 transcriptions. 00704325 $16.95

signature licks

Each Signature Licks book/cassette pak explores the sty and technique of each artist. The books contain full performance notes and an overview of each artist or group's styl The cassettes feature playing tips and techniques, as well playing examples at a slower tempo. These paks are d signed for beginners through advanced players.

THE BEST OF ERIC CLAPTON
12 of his greatest. 00673390 $16.95

IRON MAIDEN — POWERSLAVE
Matching folio to the LP. 00674100 $16.95